What Readers Are Saying Abou

D0760421

Mike has been around the block with S̲ ... the toolset
intimately. Just as importantly, he's seen firsthand how it's used on real
projects. Those two aspects come together in this book with the fundamen-
tals of source control with Subversion, guided by real-world, pragmatic (of
course!) experience. As a Subversion user and occasional noob, this is the
book I want to guide me day to day and dig me out of those irksome holes.

> ► **Jim Webber**
> Author, *REST in Practice*

I really like the organization of the book. I found *Pragmatic Guide to Subversion* to be very easy to read, and it really gets the information across in
an engaging way. This book is clear, concise, and comprehensive. It's an
indispensable reference for anyone working with Subversion.

> ► **Ian Bourke**
> Independent software developer, UK

A good digest of Subversion's capabilities. The author's writing style is
terse yet conversational, and the book progressed nicely from basic topics
to those more advanced. Overall, I think the book is an excellent follow-up
to *Pragmatic Version Control Using Subversion*.

> ► **Graham Nash**
> Retlang, Message-based concurrency in .NET

This is a book worth having since the "full" Pragmatic Subversion book is
too big for every developer on a team to read. I was a fan of Mike's original
Subversion book, and he's carried on the style into this pocket reference.
This is a book I recommend.

> ► **Mike Roberts**
> Senior software engineer, DRW Trading Group

Pragmatic Guide to Subversion has everything I needed to get up and running with SVN on my Mac. Being new to Mac OS X, it was a welcome surprise to have examples in multiple operating systems.

> ► **Michael Raczynski**
> Software architect, Canada

Pragmatic Guide to Subversion

Pragmatic Guide to Subversion

Mike Mason

The Pragmatic Bookshelf
Raleigh, North Carolina   Dallas, Texas

Pragmatic Bookshelf

Our Pragmatic courses, workshops, and other products can help you and your team create better software and have more fun. For more information, as well as the latest Pragmatic titles, please visit us at http://www.pragprog.com.

The team that produced this book includes:

Editor:	Jackie Carter
Indexing:	Potomac Indexing, LLC
Copy edit:	Kim Wimpsett
Layout:	Steve Peter
Production:	Janet Furlow
Customer support:	Ellie Callahan
International:	Juliet Benda

ISBN-10: 1-934356-61-1

ISBN-13: 978-1-934356-61-6

Printed on acid-free paper.

P1.0 printing, October 2010

Version: 2010-10-29

Contents

Acknowledgments

Every book—even a shorter one like this Pragmatic Guide—represents an incredible amount of work by a large group of people. As an author, my contribution is only a fraction of the effort that's required to get a book into the hands of readers, and I'd like to thank everyone else involved.

First and foremost, I'd like to thank my family for supporting me while writing another book. I'm a new dad with a young son at home, and despite my best efforts to write faster, our daughter arrived too before I finished the book. So, to my wife, Michelle, and her mom, Pat, thanks for taking care of the kids and letting me have those Sundays in the office writing the book. To Ben and Natalie, thanks for not being too upset when "Daddy working!" I promise to always come home.

Next, the Pragmatic Guide series idea came from Travis Swicegood, author of the excellent *Pragmatic Version Control Using Git* [Swi08]. I really liked the idea of a "get up to speed fast" Subversion book, so thank you, Travis. The folks at Pragmatic Bookshelf were super-awesome to work with as usual, although the operation is a lot bigger than when I did the original Subversion book five years ago. To Jackie Carter, my editor, thanks for keeping me on track and (nicely) pushing me to finish. I always felt that you had lots of time for me, and the book is much better as a result. To Dave and Andy, thanks for building a nontraditional publishing company that creates great books and gives authors a good deal.

A small army of people helped with the technical content in the book. To my reviewers, Rob Baillie, Ian Bourke, Kevin Gisi, Leesa Hicks, Michael Raczynski, Mike Roberts, and Graham Nash, thank you very much indeed. Your feedback has made this book better, and your encouraging words helped me finish the writing. To my fellow ThoughtWorks authors, especially Martin Fowler and Jonathan McCracken, thank you for being a sounding board while I worked on the book.

Finally, I'd like to thank you, the reader, for choosing this book. I hope you enjoy reading it—I certainly enjoyed writing it.

Introduction

Subversion is a wildly popular open source version control system, available for free over the Internet. Subversion is widely considered the de facto standard[1] for version control tools, even though such a thing is difficult to measure, and as a developer, you are likely to encounter Subversion as part of your work.

Subversion is a mature, fully featured system that is commonly used by both commercial and open source development teams. You can buy commercial support and consulting services to help you install, configure, and use Subversion. If you don't want the hassle of running a Subversion server, you can get a third party to do it for you, at a low cost or even for free.

Subversion is a *centralized* version control system, meaning that it uses a central server to store files and enable team collaboration. Clients can work disconnected from the network—on an airplane, for example—and need a network connection only if they actually want to commit changes to the server. This traditional centralized model assumes that development teams have reasonable network connectivity to the server. In contrast, some newer *decentralized* version control systems use a model where each user acts kind of like a server. Users can swap changes between each other without needing a central server. Most organizations will be fine with the centralized model used by Subversion, but it's worth being aware that other collaboration styles are possible.

Subversion is popular because it has all the features that programmers need and very few extra bells and whistles. It just does version control, and it does it well.

Subversion can track version information for directories and metadata, as well as files. Treating directories as first-class objects means that Subversion can track history across directory moves and renames, unlike some older version

---

1. Determining the exact market share for Subversion is difficult, but several online polls rate Subversion more popular than any other version control tool. Martin Fowler suggests that within the Agile/XP community, only Subversion, Git, and Mercurial would be recommended: http://martinfowler.com/bliki/VersionControlTools.html.

control systems. Every file and directory can have arbitrary metadata associated with it using Subversion *properties*.

Committing a change is *atomic*, similar to committing to a database. Either the whole commit succeeds or is rolled back; other users never see a half-finished commit. As part of the atomic commit process, Subversion groups all your changes into a *revision* (sometimes called a *changeset*) and assigns a *revision number* to the change, unlike older systems that apply a revision number to each individual file. By grouping changes to multiple files into a single logical unit, developers are able to better organize and track their changes.

Subversion has cheap *branches* and *tags* that can be created almost instantly. Branches are used to distinguish different lines of development, most commonly to separate code that is in production vs. code that is being actively developed. Tags are used to "mark" the state of the code at a particular point in time so that state can be re-created later. Subversion also supports *merge tracking*, which helps automatically merge changes between branches.

Subversion is a truly multiplatform tool. You can run Subversion on Windows, Linux, OS X, and many other flavors of Unix. Each of these operating systems is considered a first-class platform by the Subversion developers, and you can run a production-strength server on any of them. A Subversion client can talk to a Subversion server even if the client and server are running on different operating systems. This is good news for anyone trying to fit Subversion into their existing infrastructure. For those evaluating Subversion, the wide choice of operating system makes things much easier since you can run a server on pretty much any spare machine.

Who Is This Book For?

Most developers have at least some experience with a source control tool and are expected to fluidly switch between tools depending on where they are working. This book was written to bridge the gap between knowing something about version control and knowing about Subversion specifically.

Pragmatic Guide to Subversion will quickly get you up to speed on Subversion. We don't spend a lot of time covering the philosophy of version control or trying to persuade you it's a good idea to store your files somewhere safe. If you are interested in a broader discussion of version control concepts and some of the reasoning behind what we do, check out *Pragmatic Version Control Using Subversion* [Mas06],[2] my previous book.

---

2.   http://pragprog.com/titles/svn2/

How to Read This Book

This book is organized into parts that each cover a portion of the Subversion software management "life cycle." Each part of the book contains some introductory pages discussing how Subversion handles particular concepts. You should read the introductions to get a feel for the overall concepts and how everything ties together, but after that, feel free to jump straight to a particular task. If you are new to source control, it's perfectly OK to read the book in order—everything will make sense and give you a good grounding in Subversion concepts.

The book is laid out as double-page spreads for each task, with a discussion of the task on the left page and the actual steps to achieve the task on the right page. This works naturally for the printed book, but many readers will be reading a digital version. If you have the screen space for it, try setting your reader to show two pages side by side to enhance your reading experience.

The parts of the book are organized as follows:

- *Part I: Getting Started* covers core Subversion concepts such as the client, server, repository, and working copies. You will learn how to choose and install a Subversion client, how to set up a local repository, and how to import your existing code into Subversion.
- *Part II: Working with Subversion* discusses daily workflow when using Subversion. You'll learn how to check out from a repository, examine or undo your changes, and commit to the repository.
- *Part III: Working with a Team* covers how to use Subversion in a team setting, how to stay in sync with your team, and how to resolve conflicts.
- *Part IV: Using the History* shows you Subversion's powerful history tools so you can understand changes made to your source tree and who made them. In some cases, you might want to undo changes that have been committed to the repository—this part shows you how.
- *Part V: Branching, Merging, and Tagging* tackles one of the more complex topics in source control. Using branches and tags, you can reliably release software to production and support it going forward.
- *Part VI: File Locking* covers Subversion's optional file locking features, which is useful if your repository contains unmergeable files such as spreadsheets or graphics.
- *Part VII: Setting Up a Server* shows you how to install a Subversion server on Linux or Windows, including securing and backing up the server. If you'd like to use third-party hosting instead of running your own server, we discuss how to do this too.

- *Part VIII: Advanced Topics* discusses Subversion features that you might not need every day but that will be important maybe once or twice when you set up a project. Included here is information on how to store multiple projects in a single Subversion repository and how to store third-party code in your own repository.

Subversion Versions

Subversion is developed by a team of programmers collaborating over the Internet. It's open source, and the Subversion team regularly releases new versions. Major versions are given numbers such as 1.6 or 1.7, with patch and bug fix releases getting numbers like 1.6.3, 1.7.1, and so on.

In general, you should always use the newest release of Subversion, because new features, bug fixes, and performance improvements are continually being made by the Subversion developers. New major versions are always backward compatible with older servers and working copies—so client version 1.5.x will work with server version 1.6.x—but the opposite is not always true.

Always upgrade all the clients on a computer at the same time. For example, if you have both the command-line client and a graphical client and you want to upgrade to Subversion 1.7, upgrade both the command-line and graphical clients at the same time. If you don't do this, one or other of the clients might complain about the working copy being in a new format that they don't understand.

In general, it's always safe to upgrade a Subversion client, but a Subversion server requires more attention. You should always ensure you have a repository backup before doing a server upgrade and that you have tested that the backup restores correctly.

Online Resources

All Pragmatic books have an online component. You can find the home page for this book here:

http://pragprog.com/titles/pg_svn/

From here you can download code and the example mBench project used throughout the book, view the book's errata, and chat with the author and other readers in a dedicated online forum.

Subversion is a mature open source system, and there is a lot of community support for it. A web search will usually turn up loads of extra information about a topic, most of which is excellent and high quality. Don't be afraid to look beyond the tasks in this book and explore for yourself.

Part I

Getting Started

To use Subversion, you need a server and a client. The server stores files inside a *repository* and makes the repository available over a network, either a LAN or the Internet. The client talks to the server and creates a *working copy* of the files from the repository. Users make changes to their files and then *commit* the changes to the repository where other members of their team can see them.

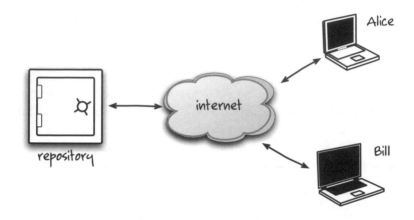

Subversion can secure network connections using SSL, the same technology used to protect credit card information online, or SSH, the secure shell used to administer Unix machines across the Internet. Subversion can store user credentials in a simple password file or integrate with an existing store such as Active Directory or LDAP.

Most users won't need to worry about administering a Subversion server, since you can easily use a third-party hosting provider over the Internet or get your company's server operations team to provision a Subversion server. If you do need to run a server yourself, it's pretty easy; see Task 33, *Installing Subversion Server*, on page 106 for more details.

Subversion was designed to be easily extended, so a wide range of different clients are available. The basic command-line client is available for most operating systems and will perform all the different Subversion functions admirably—you might never need more than the command-line client. For some operations, it's nice to have a GUI to make things easier, so a wide range of graphical Subversion clients are also available. Doing check-ins, merges, and history browsing can particularly benefit from a GUI.

For tasks in this book, we are using the command-line client on Ubuntu Linux. The client is very similar on Windows and Mac, and all the command-line examples will work on all three operating systems. We've chosen the TortoiseSVN graphical client for Windows and the Cornerstone graphical client for Mac OS X. All of the tasks in the book include instructions on how to do the job using the graphical clients as well as the command-line client.

If you are using an integrated development environment (IDE) such as IntelliJ, Eclipse, or Xcode, you'll find that it supports Subversion out of the box. You can update working copies, fix conflicts, commit changes, and view history without leaving the IDE. Other IDEs such as Visual Studio require a plug-in to work with Subversion, but once you've installed the plug-in, you can work with Subversion seamlessly. If you're using an IDE, it's definitely worth checking out its support for Subversion. Good IDE integration for your source control tool can be a significant productivity enhancement.

Covered in this part:

- First you'll need to install a Subversion client. If you're on Linux or prefer a command-line client, refer to Task 1, *Installing a Command-Line Client*, on page 6. Windows users should refer to Task 2, *Installing a Graphical Client on Windows*, on page 8. Mac users should read Task 3, *Installing a Graphical Client on Mac OS X*, on page 10.

- If you don't have a Subversion repository already set up, Task 4, *Creating a Local Repository*, on page 12 will show you how to set up a local file repository for learning Subversion.

- Once you have a Subversion repository in place, refer to Task 5, *Creating an Empty Project*, on page 14 to start off with a blank project in your repository.

- If you already have source code that you'd like to store in Subversion, Task 6, *Creating a Project from an Existing Source Tree*, on page 16 shows you how to import your existing source code into Subversion.

Let's jump right into installing Subversion.

1 Installing a Command-Line Client

We recommend installing the command-line client even if you intend to do most of your work with a graphical client. It's useful to have the basic functionality available as a fallback, in case you can't get the GUI to do what you want.

Installing the client on Windows is fairly straightforward; just double-click the installer from CollabNet, and it will set everything up for you. You can get the Windows command-line client from other distributors than CollabNet, but the installers generally aren't as friendly.

Installing Subversion on the Mac is somewhat complicated because you have several options. Depending on which release of OS X you're using, you may already have the command-line Subversion client. Snow Leopard comes with Subversion 1.6, Leopard comes with Subversion 1.4, and older releases of OS X don't come with Subversion at all. If you're using anything older than Snow Leopard, you should upgrade to the latest release of Subversion.

If you have MacPorts or Fink installed on your system, then you can use their package managers to install Subversion. If you haven't heard of these tools, don't worry; they're just a convenient way to get Unix tools on the Mac.

Subversion is available as part of the official Ubuntu distribution, so it might already be installed on your system. If not, just use the apt package manager to install it. Graphical Subversion clients are available for Ubuntu such as Subcommander or RapidSVN, but for the purposes of this book, we'll stick to the command-line client.

If you're more comfortable using the Ubuntu desktop than the command line, you can also install Subversion using Synaptic, Ubuntu's graphical package manager.

Once you've installed the Subversion command-line client, you should be able to open a command prompt and run Subversion commands. To see what release of Subversion is installed, run svn --version. You should see something like this:

```
prompt> svn --version
svn, version 1.6.12 (r955767)
   compiled Jun 23 2010, 10:32:19
```

Make sure you have Subversion 1.6 or newer. The working copy format changed in Subversion 1.5 and again in 1.6, and older clients cannot use the new formats.

▶ Install the Windows command-line client from CollabNet.

Visit CollabNet,[3] and download the command-line client. Once it's downloaded, double-click the file to start the installer. If you're not interested in running a Subversion server, uncheck the svnserve and Apache options during the install.

▶ Install the Mac command-line client from CollabNet.

Visit CollabNet,[4] and download its universal binaries for OS X. After you've run the installer, add the following line to ~/.profile:

```
export PATH=/opt/subversion/bin:$PATH
```

If you're using MacPorts, you can use it to install Subversion:

```
prompt> sudo port install subversion
```

If you're using Fink, you can use it to install Subversion:

```
prompt> sudo fink install svn-client
```

▶ Install the Ubuntu client.

```
prompt> sudo apt-get update
prompt> sudo apt-get install subversion
```

Alternatively, click System > Administration > Synaptic Package Manager to start Synaptic. Type *subversion* into the search box to show just Subversion-related packages. Click the box next to the subversion package, and then select "Mark for installation." Choose to mark any other packages that are required. Click the Apply button to install the Subversion packages.

Related Tasks

- Task 2, *Installing a Graphical Client on Windows*, on the next page
- Task 3, *Installing a Graphical Client on Mac OS X*, on page 10
- Task 33, *Installing Subversion Server*, on page 106

---

3. http://www.collab.net/downloads/subversion/svn1.5.html
4. http://www.open.collab.net/downloads/community/

2 Installing a Graphical Client on Windows

TortoiseSVN is an excellent Subversion client for Windows that integrates directly into Windows Explorer. Once Tortoise is installed, you can right-click anywhere in a Windows Explorer window and get context-sensitive Subversion options. If you right-click in a directory that isn't a Subversion working copy, Tortoise will offer to let you check it out from a repository. If you right-click a directory that is a working copy, Tortoise will offer to let you update or commit. If you right-click a file inside a working copy, Tortoise will offer to show history for the file, and so on.

Throughout the rest of the book, we'll use a shorthand to denote choosing Tortoise menu options, rather than showing screenshots all the time. To indicate that you should right-click to get the context menu and then click TortoiseSVN and then Show Log, we will use the abbreviation

TortoiseSVN > Show Log.

Tortoise shows its context-sensitive options both immediately on the context menu and within the TortoiseSVN flyout menu. Tortoise lets you move frequently used operations from the flyout to the context menu so you can save yourself a click or two. To do this, choose TortoiseSVN > Settings, and then select Context Menu. Select the box next to each operation that you'd like available directly on the context menu.

Tortoise needs a Subversion repository in order to do anything useful. If you have a repository already set up, you just need to know the repository URL, and you can get going. If you are trying Subversion for yourself and need to set up a local repository for testing, see Task 4, *Creating a Local Repository*, on page 12.

► Install the Tortoise graphical client.

Visit tortoisesvn.net,[5] and download TortoiseSVN. Tortoise is integrated with Windows Explorer, so you should reboot your system once the installer finishes.

Once it's installed, you can right-click inside any Windows Explorer window to get a context-sensitive TortoiseSVN menu.

🔍	Show log
🔍	Repo-browser
🔍	Check for modifications
🔍	Revision graph
🔍	Resolved...
🔍	Update to revision...
🔍	Revert...
🔍	Clean up
🔒	Get lock...
🔒	Release lock
🏷	Branch/tag...
🔀	Switch...
Y	Merge...
📤	Export...
🔀	Relocate...
✛	Add...
🧩	Create patch...
🧩	Apply patch...
🔍	Properties
🐢	Settings
?	Help
🐢	About

Related Tasks

- Task 1, *Installing a Command-Line Client*, on page 6
- Task 33, *Installing Subversion Server*, on page 106

---

5. http://tortoisesvn.net/downloads

3 Installing a Graphical Client on Mac OS X

Cornerstone is one of several Subversion clients available for the Mac. It has a nice, clean interface and a similar feel to other OS X applications. Cornerstone is commercial software, so you need to buy a license to use it longer than its free 14-day trial period.

The Cornerstone window has several sections. Along the top is a *button bar* with icons for the most common Subversion operations. To the left is a column containing the *working copy source list* and the *repository source list*. In the center is the main working window, which can show a *working copy browser*, a *commit view*, and a range of other information depending on what you currently have selected. To the right is the *inspector*, which shows more detail about the currently selected item.

If you already know the URL for the repository you want to access, click the Add Repository... button or click the small + button at the top of the repository source list. Most repositories will be either HTTP or SVN Server; ask your administrator if you're not sure. When adding a repository, it's best to omit the trunk directory from the end of the URL so that you can see the top-level directories and work with them.

If you don't know the URL for your repository, you should ask the person in charge of your project. If that person is you, use the instructions in Task 5, *Creating an Empty Project*, on page 14 to set up your project. If you'd like to set up a local repository to get going quickly, see Task 4, *Creating a Local Repository*, on page 12.

Adding a repository to the repository source list doesn't actually copy any files to your computer; we'll do that in Task 7, *Checking Out a Working Copy*, on page 24. The rest of the Cornerstone examples in this book assume you have added the Subversion repository for your project.

► Install the Cornerstone graphical client.

Visit the Cornerstone website,[6] and download Cornerstone. Double-click the disk image, and drag the Cornerstone application into your Applications folder.

When running Cornerstone, you'll be greeted with the main window, as shown here:

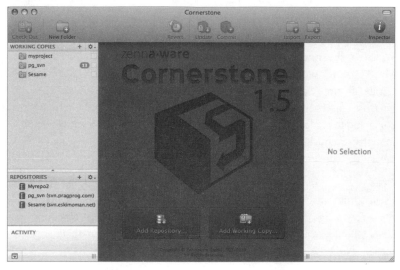

Related Tasks

- Task 1, *Installing a Command-Line Client*, on page 6
- Task 33, *Installing Subversion Server*, on page 106

---

6. http://www.zennaware.com/cornerstone/

4 Creating a Local Repository

Most people using Subversion don't need to worry about creating or maintaining a repository since it's an administrative task usually performed by a server administrator or Unix guru. If you don't have access to one of these people or if you'd like to experiment with your own repository, you can use what's called a *local repository*.

A local repository needs to live on your hard drive somewhere. For Windows, this might be a dedicated directory on the C: drive; for Unix and Mac OS X, it's probably somewhere in your home directory. Once you have created an empty directory, you need to tell Subversion to initialize a repository in that directory. Command-line users should use the svnadmin command to achieve this. Tortoise users should right-click the directory to initialize a repository. Cornerstone users should use the Cornerstone GUI to create the repository.

Once you have initialized the repository, you can start using it, but you'll need to tell Subversion where to find the repository. This is where the repository *base URL* is needed. The base URL for a local repository always starts with file:// and ends with the path within the file system to get to your repository directory.

You can turn a local repository into a networked repository by running a Subversion server and pointing it at the repository directory. You can find more details in Task 33, *Installing Subversion Server*, on page 106.

► Create a base directory for the repository, and then initialize it.

```
prompt> mkdir -p ~/svn/repos
prompt> svnadmin create ~/svn/repos
```

The base URL for your local repository is file:///home/myuser/svn/repos.

► Create a local repository using Tortoise.

Using Windows Explorer, create an empty directory for your repository. Something such as C:\Subversion\Repos will work.

Right-click inside the new directory, and choose TortoiseSVN > Create repository here.

The base URL for your local repository is file:///C:/Subversion/Repos.

► Create a local repository using Cornerstone.

Choose File > Add Repository..., or click the plus icon in the repository source list.

Select the File Repository button at the top, and click Create a New Repository. Click the Where drop-down, and choose the folder in which you want to create your repository. Usually a dedicated svn directory within your home directory will work.

Enter a repository name in the "Create as" box. This is the actual directory where your new repository will be stored.

Click the Compatibility drop-down, and choose 1.6. Finally, click the Add button to create the local repository.

The base URL for your local repository is file:///Users/myuser/svn/repos.

Related Tasks

- Task 34, *Creating a Repository*, on page 108
- Task 5, *Creating an Empty Project*, on the following page
- Task 36, *Using Third-Party Subversion Hosting*, on page 112

5 Creating an Empty Project

Most Subversion users won't often need to *create* a project—that's usually done by a systems administrator or a third-party hosting company. If the project is already set up and you know the URL, you can jump to Task 7, *Checking Out a Working Copy*, on page 24.

Subversion uses directories as its basic unit of organization, dividing the repository into different projects. By convention, all Subversion projects have trunk, tags, and branches directories directly within the project's root directory. If you had two projects, Kithara and Sesame, you would end up with the following directory structure:

- /Kithara/trunk
- /Kithara/tags
- /Kithara/branches
- /Sesame/trunk
- /Sesame/tags
- /Sesame/branches

The trunk directory is where all the main development action happens and is usually the directory you will check out if you want to work on the project. Remember to specify the trunk when checking out; otherwise, you'll get the trunk, all the tags, and all the branches! This could be quite a lot of stuff and usually isn't what you want.

The tags directory is used to store named snapshots of the project. For example, when creating a production release, the team will tag the code that goes into the release. In the future this can help you re-create the code that was shipped so that the team can find bugs and fix problems.

The branches directory is used when you want to pursue different lines of development. A good example would be creating a branch for a production release. Development on the branch can focus on producing a stable release, while the trunk can continue to be used to develop new features.

Although you can store multiple projects within a single Subversion repository, some people use a different repository for each project. This allows some increased flexibility, for example having different sets of users or a different backup schedule between projects, but at the cost of extra administration overhead because each repository needs to be configured and backed up individually. If you are using a repository-per-project style for managing your Subversion projects, the trunk, tags, and branches directories will be at the root of each project's repository.

▶ Create a base directory for the project.

If you are sharing a single repository between multiple projects, create a directory within the repository for your new project.

```
prompt> svn mkdir -m "Make base directory" \
                http://svn.mycompany.com/myproject
```

▶ Create a repository for the project.

If you are using a separate repository for each project, follow the steps in Task 34, *Creating a Repository*, on page 108 to create a repository for your project.

▶ Create trunk, tags, and branches directories.

```
prompt> svn mkdir -m "Initial setup" \
                http://svn.mycompany.com/myproject/trunk
prompt> svn mkdir -m "Initial setup" \
                http://svn.mycompany.com/myproject/tags
prompt> svn mkdir -m "Initial setup" \
                http://svn.mycompany.com/myproject/branches
```

▶ Use Tortoise to create directories.

Right-click inside any Explorer window, and choose TortoiseSVN > Repo-browser. Enter the URL for your repository, for example http://svn.mycompany.com/. Tortoise will show you a repository browser where you can manipulate your repository. Right-click, and choose "Create folder" as necessary to create all the directories you need for your project.

▶ Use Cornerstone to create a project.

Select your repository from the repository source list. Cornerstone will show its repository browser in the main window. Ctrl+click the main window, and choose "New folder in MyRepo...." Enter a name for the project, and select the box to create top-level directories for the project. Enter a log message describing your change, and then click Continue to create your project.

Related Tasks

- Task 34, *Creating a Repository*, on page 108
- Task 36, *Using Third-Party Subversion Hosting*, on page 112

6 ▎ Creating a Project from an Existing Source Tree

Often when creating a project in version control, you will already have some files that are the starting point for the project. This is especially true if you are starting to use Subversion on a project that didn't previously have version control or you are moving from another version control system. Even if you have done only an afternoon's work on a new project, you are likely to have a local directory that represents a good starting point for the project. Subversion's import functionality will create a project inside your repository using your local directory and its contents. Once imported, a copy of your files will be safely stored on the Subversion server.

Before importing anything, you should make sure you have cleaned up any temporary files or other garbage that might be lying around. Most build tools and IDEs have an option to "clean" your project—it's worth doing this and generally having a look around to make sure you only import the stuff you really want. If you accidentally import a file that you don't want, you can delete it from the repository, but because Subversion stores the history of all the files it has ever known about, that file will still be in the repository taking up space. This isn't a big deal for small files, but if you have large binaries such as debugging symbols, you really should clean them up before doing an import.

Doing an svn import or using one of the GUI tools grabs an entire directory full of files and checks it into your Subversion repository in one fell swoop. As long as the repository is valid, Subversion will create any directories it needs along the way. If you haven't yet created a trunk folder, for example, Subversion will create it for you.

▶ Clean up your existing source tree.

Delete any temporary files or build artifacts from your source directory. Your IDE might have a Clean Up option, or if you're using a command-line build tool, you should run make clean.[7]

Check for hidden files or directories, such as .cvs administrative directories from the CVS source control system. Remove anything that you don't want imported into the new Subversion project.

▶ Import the whole tree to your project directory.

```
prompt> cd work/myproject-to-import
prompt> svn import -m "Initial import" \
                  http://svn.mycompany.com/myproject/trunk
```

▶ Import the whole tree using Tortoise.

Using Windows Explorer, right-click the directory you want to import, and choose TortoiseSVN > Import.... Enter the repository URL for your project (make sure to include the trunk directory at the end of the URL), and enter a message describing what you're importing. Click OK to complete the import.

▶ Import the whole tree using Cornerstone.

Select your repository from the repository source list. Ctrl+click in the base of the repository browser, and choose Import....

In the file dialog box, browse to the directory you want to import, select it, and click the Open button. In the Import As text box, enter myproject/trunk as the directory to import to. Click Import, enter a log message, and Cornerstone will import your files.

Use the repository browser to navigate to your newly imported trunk directory. Create tags and branches directories next to the trunk.

Related Tasks

• Task 5, *Creating an Empty Project*, on page 14

---

7. Substitute the build tool of your choice, such as ant, nant, maven, msbuild, or rake.

Part II

Working with Subversion

Now that we have Subversion installed and a repository set up, we can begin doing useful work. While Subversion is designed to enable team collaboration, you can also use it individually. If you are programming or authoring on your own, the diff, history, and commit tools can help you organize your work. You can also use Subversion as a kind of safe "backup" copy for your files.

In this section, you'll see how to get a working copy of the files from Subversion. After you make changes to your files, you commit the changes to the repository. We'll also cover renaming and moving files and directories.

In this section and for the rest of the book, we'll be using an example project called *mBench*. mBench is a simple benchmarking tool for MongoDB, one of a new generation of nonrelational databases (sometimes known as "NoSQL" databases). Mongo is a document-oriented database with very different performance and reliability characteristics than a traditional SQL database. Before using Mongo in production, we'd like to make sure it meets our needs for speed and reliability. mBench will contain Java code to exercise Mongo, documentation detailing things we find out about how to best use Mongo, and other artifacts such as performance testing results.

The complete source code for mBench is available as part of the code download for this book. The code, errata, and forums are available from the Pragmatic Bookshelf at http://pragprog.com/titles/pg_ svn. For all the tasks involving mBench, we assume that it's available from a repository at http://svn.mycompany.com/mbench. This URL isn't real, so you should substitute your own repository URL when working with the examples.

Covered in this part:

- To edit files stored in Subversion, you need to first get a copy of the files on your machine. Task 7, *Checking Out a Working Copy*, on page 24 shows you how.

- Task 8, *Seeing What You've Changed*, on page 26 covers how Subversion shows the edits you have made to files. Task 9, *Seeing What You've Changed Using Tortoise*, on page 28 and Task 10, *Seeing What You've Changed Using Cornerstone*, on page 30 show you how to examine changes using GUI tools.

- Once you have made your changes, you need to commit them to the repository. I describe the commit process in Task 11, *Committing Changes*, on page 32.

- Task 12, *Adding Files and Directories*, on page 34 covers how to add new items to your repository, while Task 13, *Removing Files and Directories*, on page 36 shows how to remove items.

- Renaming and moving items is covered in Task 14, *Moving and Renaming Files and Directories*, on page 38.

- If you make a local change that you'd like to undo, follow the instructions in Task 15, *Reverting Working Copy Changes*, on page 40.

- Subversion allows you to ignore temporary files; Task 16, *Ignoring Files*, on page 42 shows you how.

Let's get started by checking out a fresh working copy.

7 Checking Out a Working Copy

You need to *check out* the files from your repository before you can access them on your computer. The files will be stored in a local directory called a *working copy*. Your Subversion client will talk to the server and copy the latest files onto your computer ready to edit. You will be asked for a username and password if your repository is secured.

Subversion projects are usually stored in a trunk directory on the server; this will be the case if you have followed the instructions in this book for creating projects. You need to specify this trunk directory as part of the repository URL from which you are checking out. If you forget, you'll end up checking out everything in the repository—branches, tags, everything—and this could end up being much more than you really wanted. After specifying the project's trunk directory, we tell Subversion that we want to check out into a local directory called mbench. If you don't include this information, Subversion will check out into a folder called trunk, which probably isn't what you want and might be quite confusing if you're working on more than one project!

After Subversion has copied files from the repository to your computer, they'll be saved in a directory known as a working copy. Inside a working copy, Subversion remembers where all the files came from, knows what revision they were when they came from the server, and can detect any changes you make to the files. Subversion uses hidden .svn directories to track all its bookkeeping information. Don't alter, delete, or otherwise mess with these directories because you could corrupt your working copy.

You need to check out from Subversion only the first time you want to work with a particular project. Once you have a working copy, you can always *update* it to get the latest files. We describe the update process in more detail in Task 17, *Updating to the Latest Revision*, on page 50.

After you check out a working copy using Cornerstone, it will automatically add the working copy as an entry in your working copy sources list. You'll need to use this entry when manipulating your working copy for the rest of the tasks in this book.

▶ Check out into a local working copy.

```
prompt> cd ~/work
prompt> svn checkout http://svn.mycompany.com/mbench/trunk mbench
```

▶ Check out using Tortoise.

Using Windows Explorer, navigate to your C:\Work directory. Right-click inside the directory, and choose SVN Checkout.... Then fill in the dialog box as follows:

▶ Check out using Cornerstone.

Select your repository in the repository source list, and then use the repository browser to navigate to the trunk directory. Ctrl+click "trunk," and choose Check Out Working Copy.... Specify where you'd like to save the new working copy, and click Check Out.

Related Tasks

- Task 5, *Creating an Empty Project*, on page 14
- Task 36, *Using Third-Party Subversion Hosting*, on page 112

8 | Seeing What You've Changed

Subversion keeps track of files in your working copy and will detect any changes you make. You can see which files or directories you've changed and even see exactly what has changed within each file. As a programmer, it's easy to get confused about what changes you have made once you're halfway through a feature, and Subversion can help keep you on track.

The status command tells Subversion to scan all the files in your working copy to see whether they've changed. Subversion uses some tricks to make this process faster, but it still has to look at each file to see whether it has changed. The scan might take a while if you have lots of files in your working copy. If you know that you've been working in only one particular directory, you can ask Subversion to tell you the status of that directory instead of the whole project, which should speed things up.

Subversion marks each file with a letter indicating its status:

A   Added in your working copy

C   Conflicted, because of an update or merge

D   Deleted in your working copy

G   Merged with changes from the repository

I   Ignored in your working copy

M   Modified in your working copy

R   Replaced in your working copy

?   Not under version control

!   Missing from your working copy (removed by non-svn command) or incomplete

The diff command asks Subversion to print out a "unified diff" for each of the files you have changed. This displays the difference between the file as you checked it out and the file after you made your changes. A plus indicates that you have added some new text to the file; a minus means you've removed some text. If you have changed several lines, you might see a group of pluses and minuses indicating that a whole "block" of your file has changed.

The command-line client isn't great at showing diffs—not surprising when a text interface is all it has to work with. The graphical Subversion clients do a much better job displaying diffs, as we'll see in the next tasks.

▶ See which files have changed in your working copy.

```
mbench> svn status
M        .idea/workspace.xml
M        src/mbench.java
```

▶ See how your files have changed.

```
prompt> svn diff src/
Index: src/mbench.java
===========================================================
--- src/mbench.java      (revision 6)
+++ src/mbench.java      (working copy)
@@ -1,10 +1,13 @@
 public class mbench {
-    public static int main(String[] args) {
+    public static void main(String[] args) {
         if(args.length != 3) {
             usage();
-            return -1;
+            return;
         }
-        return 0;
+
+        String dbHost = args[0];
+        long docCount = Long.parseLong(args[1]);
+        long runTime = Integer.parseInt(args[2]);
     }

     private static void usage() {
```

Related Tasks

- Task 21, *Viewing the Log*, on page 62
- Task 9, *Seeing What You've Changed Using Tortoise*, on the next page
- Task 10, *Seeing What You've Changed Using Cornerstone*, on page 30
- Task 15, *Reverting Working Copy Changes*, on page 40

9 Seeing What You've Changed Using Tortoise

The Tortoise Check for modifications... command can be used anywhere inside a working copy and will show any changes you have made. Similar to the command-line client, it will do its work faster if you know you're only interested in changes in a particular directory. Each file listed is color coded as well as having its state listed in the "text status" column.

There are a number of checkboxes that control how Tortoise shows changes:

Show unversioned files
> Shows any new files that haven't yet been added to Subversion. It's a good idea to keep this option selected so you don't forget to add new files when committing to the repository.

Show unmodified files
> Useful only on really small projects, this will show files that *haven't* been modified.

Show ignored files
> Not usually very useful, this will show any files that Subversion is currently ignoring. For more information on ignored files, see Task 16, *Ignoring Files*, on page 42.

Show items in externals
> If you are using Subversion *externals* to pull items from another repository URL into your working copy, this option will show any changes to those files. See Task 44, *Using Externals*, on page 132 for more information on externals. You should usually keep this option selected.

Show properties
> Shows changes to file properties. You can usually keep this option deselected unless you're specifically changing file properties.

You can right-click changed files to see a context-sensitive menu for each item. You can view the recent history, undo your changes, open the file, and so on. If you double-click a changed file or right-click and choose "Compare with base," Tortoise will pop up a graphical diff window showing the changes. By default Tortoise uses TortoiseMerge to show diffs, but you can configure it to use your favorite diff tool.

▶ See which files have changed in your working copy.

Right-click the base directory of your working copy, and choose TortoiseSVN > Check for modifications.... Tortoise will show a window like this:

▶ See how your files have changed.

In the Tortoise modified files window, double-click a file that you've changed. Tortoise will pop open a diff window showing the changes to that file.

Related Tasks

• Task 21, *Viewing the Log*, on page 62
• Task 15, *Reverting Working Copy Changes*, on page 40

10 Seeing What You've Changed Using Cornerstone

When you select a working copy from the working copy sources list, Cornerstone automatically checks for changes and updates its file list accordingly. By default Cornerstone will show all the files in your working copy, which might be too much to look through for anything beyond a small project. Select the Changed view to show only files that have changed or are new.

Modified files are shown with a little M icon to the right of their name. New files are shown with a yellow question-mark icon, added files are shown with a green A icon, and deleted files are shown with a red D icon.

To see exactly what has changed in a particular file, select it and click Compare with BASE on the menu bar. This shows the changes that you have made since you last updated the file from the repository. You can also use Compare with HEAD to show the differences between your version of the file and the latest one in the repository.

► See which files have changed in your working copy.

Select your working copy from the working copy sources list. Cornerstone
will show you the working copy browser in the main window. Click the
Changed button at the top of the browser to show just files that have changes.

► See how your files have changed.

Select a changed file, and click the Compare with BASE button at the
bottom of the working copy browser. Cornerstone will use its built-in
graphical diff tool to show you how the file has changed:

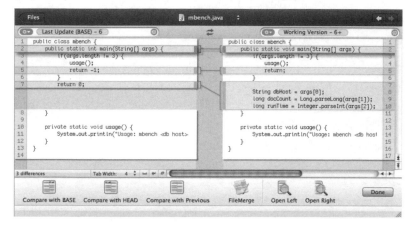

Related Tasks

11 Committing Changes

Once you are happy with the changes you have made, you should *commit* them back into the repository. Changes committed into the repository are available to everyone else on your project and are stored securely on your Subversion server. Committing changes is sometimes also known as *checking in* to the repository; these two terms mean the same thing and can be used interchangeably.

Any time you commit a change into the repository, Subversion will ask for a *commit message*. Your changes, along with the commit message, then become a *revision* within the Subversion repository. You should always try to make your commit messages meaningful—they can be used later by someone else (or more often yourself!) to figure out the intent of the changes. It's always better to describe *why* you made the changes instead of *what* the changes are. Subversion can always show the actual content of the change; it can't help someone understand the intent of the change.

If you are working on a software project, you should always update from the repository and run a build before committing changes (see Task 17, *Updating to the Latest Revision*, on page 50). This ensures that your changes will work with the latest code from the repository and that you haven't broken anything. Your colleagues will thank you for being so conscientious.

If you don't want to commit all the changes from your working copy, you can tell Subversion which files or directories to commit by specifying them on the command line or choosing them in your GUI. Be extra careful when doing this, however. If you are a programmer working on code and you check in only half your changes, it's likely what you checked in will not work for someone else.

When using Tortoise, the commit window acts a little like the "Check for modifications..." window. You can type a commit message into the top portion and see all the changed files in the lower portion. Double-clicking any changed file allows you to review the diff. Unchecking a file will cause it not to be committed.

Committing using Cornerstone shows a window listing the changed files and asking for a commit message. If you want to review exactly what you've changed, double-click a modified file to show an exact graphical diff. Unchecking a file will stop Cornerstone from committing it.

▶ Commit your changes back into the repository.

```
mbench> svn commit -m "Now parsing command-line options"
```

▶ Commit using Tortoise.

Right-click inside the base of your working copy, and choose SVN Commit.... Tortoise will show a commit window like this:

▶ Commit using Cornerstone.

Select your project from the working copy sources list, and then click the Commit icon on the menu bar. Cornerstone will prompt you for a commit message and show a list of modified files; click Commit Changes to finish your commit.

Related Tasks

- Task 8, *Seeing What You've Changed*, on page 26
- Task 17, *Updating to the Latest Revision*, on page 50

12 | Adding Files and Directories

Subversion will notice new files and directories within your working copy, but it won't automatically add them to the repository. Adding items to the repository is a two-step process; first you tell Subversion you want to *add* the items to your working copy, and then you *commit* your changes to actually upload the items to the repository.

This two-step process is important. When you create a new file, it won't be very useful to anyone else until you add content to the file, but you also need to remember to add the file to Subversion. If you wait until you finish your programming task, you might forget to add the file. With Subversion, you can go ahead and add the file to your working copy right away; this won't change anything on the Subversion server, and no one else can see the file yet, but when you finish your work and commit your changes, the new file will be uploaded to the repository. This is sometimes called *scheduling* files for addition to the repository.

The command-line client will add the files or directories you specify. When adding a directory, the command-line client will recursively add any files and directories within the directory you're adding.

When using Tortoise to add files, if you choose to add a directory, Tortoise will show you a complete list of the contents of the directory. If there are files you don't want to add, just uncheck them before clicking OK.

If you're using Cornerstone to add a directory, clicking the Add button will add the directory but not its contents. If you want to add a directory and its contents, click and hold the Add button, and then choose Add to Working Copy with Contents.

If you schedule files or directories for addition to the repository but haven't actually committed your changes, you can change your mind by *reverting* the addition. For more information, see Task 15, *Reverting Working Copy Changes*, on page 40.

► Add new files and directories from your working copy.

```
mbench> svn add README.txt docs/
mbench> svn commit -m "Adding docs folder for documentation"
```

► Add files using Tortoise.

Using Windows Explorer, navigate to the file or directory you want to add. Right-click, and choose TortoiseSVN > Add....

Commit your changes by right-clicking the base of your working copy and choosing SVN Commit....

► Add files using Cornerstone.

Select your project from the working copy sources list, and click the Changed button. Find the new file—it should have a yellow question-mark icon to its right—and select it. Click the Add button in the bottom toolbar.

Commit your changes by clicking Commit on the top toolbar.

Related Tasks

- Task 8, *Seeing What You've Changed*, on page 26
- Task 11, *Committing Changes*, on page 32
- Task 15, *Reverting Working Copy Changes*, on page 40

13 | Removing Files and Directories

Similar to adding items, deleting items from the repository is a two-step process; first you tell Subversion you want to delete the items from your working copy, and then you commit your changes to the repository. Until you commit the change, the delete won't happen on the server.

As with adding items, this two-step process is important because you are likely to want to commit your delete along with some changes to other files. For example, if you're using an IDE to manage your source code and want to delete a class, the change consists of both removing the class file and changing the IDE project file to no longer reference the file. You should commit both these changes in one go.

When deleting a directory, Subversion will recursively delete any files and directories within the directory you're deleting. Subversion won't actually remove the directory *structure*, however, because Subversion still needs to access its administrative data in the hidden .svn directories. Don't delete these directories yourself—once you commit your changes, Subversion will clean up the empty directory structure. The command-line clients, Tortoise, and Cornerstone all behave like this, so don't worry if you see empty directories lying around after a delete.

If you schedule files or directories for deletion from the repository but haven't yet committed your changes, you can change your mind and *revert* the delete. Reverting a delete restores the deleted files and directories to your working copy. For more information, see Task 15, *Reverting Working Copy Changes*, on page 40.

▶ Delete files and directories from your working copy.

```
prompt> svn delete src/app/Widget.cs src/app/utils
prompt> svn commit -m "Deleted Widget class and utils package"
```

▶ Delete files and directories using Tortoise.

Right-click a file or directory, and choose TortoiseSVN > Delete.

Commit your changes by right-clicking the base of your working copy and choosing SVN Commit....

▶ Delete files and directories using Cornerstone.

Select your project from the working copy sources list, and click the All button in the browser. Find the file or directory you want to delete, Cmd+click the item, and choose Delete....

Select the base of your working copy in the browser, and then click Commit on the toolbar to commit your changes.

Related Tasks

14 Moving and Renaming Files and Directories

Moving and renaming are almost the same within Subversion.[8] To *rename* a file or directory, you just *move* it so that it has a new name but is in the same location. To move a file or directory to a new location, specify the destination directory. You can also move and rename at the same time by specifying a renamed file or directory in a new location.

Moving or renaming an item is a two-phase process, similar to adding or deleting; first you tell Subversion you want to move or rename the items, and then you commit your changes to the repository.

If you're looking closely, Subversion tracks a move or rename as an add of the item with a new name or in a new location and a delete of the old item. Internally Subversion tracks where the new item came from so you can follow history across moves and renames.

The Subversion command line accepts move, mv, and ren as aliases for rename.

Tortoise has an excellent interface for moving files and directories once you discover the "right-drag" feature. Tortoise allows you to move, or move and rename, in one operation. To right-drag a file, place your mouse pointer over it, and click and hold the right mouse button. Still holding the right mouse button, drag the file to its new location, and then let go of the mouse button.

Cornerstone has an intuitive interface for moving files and directories: simply drag the item to a new position using the working copy browser. As you drop the item in a new location, Cornerstone will offer to let you change the name. If you want to keep the same name, just hit Enter, and Cornerstone will move the item without renaming it.

---

8. Subversion is heavily influenced by Unix, where there is no *rename* command—you just move the item to a new name to rename it.

▶ Rename a file using the command-line client.

```
prompt> svn mv README.txt 001-README.txt
A         001-README.txt
D         README.txt
prompt> svn commit -m "README now shows first in directory"
```

▶ Move a file using the command-line client.

```
prompt> svn mv src/app/Widget.cs src/app/util/
prompt> svn commit -m "Moved Widget class into util package"
```

▶ Rename a file using Tortoise.

Right-click a file or directory, and choose TortoiseSVN > Rename....

Commit your changes by right-clicking the base of your working copy and choosing SVN Commit....

▶ Move a file using Tortoise.

Using Windows Explorer, right-drag the file to a different location in your working copy, and choose "SVN Move versioned item(s) here."

Commit your changes by right-clicking the base of your working copy and choosing SVN Commit....

▶ Rename a file using Cornerstone.

Using the working copy browser, select the file you want to rename. Wait a moment, and then click the file again. The filename will become editable; type a new name for the file, and hit Enter.

Click Commit on the toolbar to commit your changes.

▶ Move a file using Cornerstone.

Using the working copy browser, drag a file to a new location. Cornerstone will offer to let you rename the file; hit Enter to confirm a new name and move the file.

Click Commit on the toolbar to commit your changes.

Related Tasks

- Task 8, *Seeing What You've Changed*, on page 26
- Task 11, *Committing Changes*, on page 32
- Task 15, *Reverting Working Copy Changes*, on the next page

15 Reverting Working Copy Changes

If you decide that you no longer want some or all the changes you have made in your working copy, you can *revert* those changes. The Subversion client will restore the files as they were when you last checked out or updated. Doing a revert doesn't get you the latest changes from the repository; you need to do an update to get those.

Subversion stores a pristine copy of each file in its hidden .svn administrative directories so it can do a revert without needing to talk to the server. This can be useful if you're editing code on a plane or from home and cannot get a network connection to the server.

Reverting a copied, moved, or renamed item within Cornerstone does not delete the newly created copy of the item. These extra files and directories will show up in the working copy browser with a yellow question mark icon next to them. Cmd+click, and choose Delete... to clean up these extra items.

Reverting working copy changes only helps you undo a work in progress. If you have committed a change and want to undo it, you'll need to look at Task 23, *Reverting a Committed Revision*, on page 66.

▶ Revert changes to specific files or directories.

```
prompt> svn revert Number.txt
prompt> svn revert -R src/util/
```

▶ Revert all the changes in your working copy.

```
prompt> cd work/mbench
prompt> svn revert -R .
```

▶ Revert changes using Tortoise.

Right-click the base directory for your working copy, and choose TortoiseSVN > Revert.... You'll see a window similar to the following:

Check the items you want to revert, and click OK.

▶ Revert changes using Cornerstone.

Select your project from the working copy sources list. In the working copy browser, select the file or directory you want to revert, and click the Revert button on the toolbar.

Related Tasks

- Task 8, *Seeing What You've Changed*, on page 26
- Task 23, *Reverting a Committed Revision*, on page 66

16 | Ignoring Files

Software development projects are complex beasts. A build tool or IDE will often create temporary files while you are working on development tasks or running a build. These temporary files are usually not useful to anyone else and should not be stored in a Subversion repository. Subversion tries to be helpful, however, and tells you that it doesn't know about any file that has not been added to the repository. These files will show with a question mark when svn status shows the working copy status and will clutter up the Tortoise and Cornerstone GUIs.

You can instruct Subversion to ignore certain files or directories by editing the svn:ignore property on the directory containing the items you want to ignore. You can find more information on properties in Task 43, *Working with Properties, on page 130*. The svn:ignore property is plain text and simply lists items to ignore, one item on each line. Wildcards are supported, so, for example, *.tmp will ignore all temporary files.

Once you have altered the svn:ignore property on the directory, you must commit the property change into the repository in order for other users to benefit; until you commit, only your working copy is ignoring the specified items. When other users update their working copies, their Subversion clients will start to ignore the items as well.

Setting svn:ignore on a directory tells Subversion to ignore particular items only in that directory. Matching items in subdirectories will not be ignored. To avoid needing to set svn:ignore on lots of directories, you should set up your project so that temporary files or binary artifacts are created in one directory. Developers often choose a build directory in the root of the working copy. Set svn:ignore to ignore the build directory, and you're done—no more temporary files cluttering up Subversion's status messages.

If you make a change to svn:ignore that you want to undo, simply revert your working copy changes. Be careful not to revert changes to files, however, because this is your work in progress! Just revert the change to the directory.

▶ Ignore files and directories using the command-line client.

```
mbench> svn status
?       test
?       out
M       .idea/workspace.xml
M       src/util/populator.java
mbench> svn propedit svn:ignore .
```

Edit the svn:ignore property so that it lists the test and out directories. Save and quit your editor.

```
mbench> svn status
svn status
 M      .
M       .idea/workspace.xml
M       src/util/populator.java
mbench> svn commit -N -m "Ignored test and out directories" .
```

▶ Ignore items using Tortoise.

Right-click the base directory for your working copy, and choose TortoiseSVN > Check for modifications. Ensure "Show unversioned files" is checked.

Right-click any file you want to ignore, and choose "Add to ignore list." Commit your changes to the repository.

▶ Ignore items using Cornerstone.

Select your project from the working copy sources list. Select the All view, and navigate to the files you want to ignore. Files that have not yet been added to your repository are indicated with a yellow question-mark icon.

Ctrl+click each file you want to ignore, and choose Ignore. Commit your changes to the repository.

Related Tasks

- Task 8, *Seeing What You've Changed*, on page 26
- Task 15, *Reverting Working Copy Changes*, on page 40

Part III

Working with a Team

Subversion is primarily a collaboration tool. Although you can use Subversion on your own, its real power comes when it enables a large team to work together on a single project. This part of the book describes how to collaborate with other members of your team as you all make changes to files stored in the repository.

For programming teams, a typical development session will involve updating to the latest version of the code, making changes as they complete development tasks, and finally committing changes to the repository. Many teams accelerate their development cycle to include multiple "update, change, commit" cycles throughout the day. This is definitely a good way to keep in sync with other people working on the project.

Subversion's collaboration model doesn't try to prevent two people from changing the same file at the same time. Usually when developers are working on different features, they're mostly working on completely different sets of files. If a team does happen to have two people working on the same file, you'll usually find that they're working on different sections of the file. Subversion can automatically merge these kinds of changes. More rarely, two developers will change exactly the same part of a file, and Subversion cannot automatically reconcile the two sets of changes. This is known as a *conflict*. Subversion 1.6 also tracks *tree conflicts*, which occur when users change files or directories in an incompatible way, such as one user renaming a file while the other user changes its contents. Subversion includes tools to help you resolve these conflicts, and we cover them in this part of the book.

Subversion's copy-modify-merge model is also known as *optimistic locking*. The alternate strategy, *pessimistic locking*, can be enabled for selected files. Task 29, *Enabling File Locking*, on page 92, describes this in more detail. Encountering lots of conflicts usually indicates that something is going wrong on your project. It might be that developers aren't talking to each other often enough and are doing overlapping work (fixing the same bug, for example). It might also indicate that your code includes files that need to be edited often—restructuring to have smaller files or classes may help.

Covered in this part:

- Staying in sync with your team is covered in Task 17, *Updating to the Latest Revision*, on page 50.

- If multiple people change the same part of a file, Subversion will report a conflict. Task 18, *Handling Conflicts*, on page 52 shows you how to resolve conflicts.

- Graphical tools give you a distinct advantage when resolving conflicts. Task 19, *Handling Conflicts Using Tortoise*, on page 54 and Task 20, *Handling Conflicts Using Cornerstone*, on page 56 describe graphical conflict-resolution in detail.

Let's start off by keeping in sync with the rest of the team.

17 | Updating to the Latest Revision

If you have multiple people working on a project, they will all be making changes and committing to the repository. Doing an update gets these changes from the repository and incorporates them into your working copy. It's a good idea to update fairly frequently; if you haven't updated for a while, then fixing any conflicts will take more time. You'll learn how to deal with conflicts in Task 18, *Handling Conflicts*, on page 52. If you have made changes in your working copy, it's still safe to do an update—Subversion will incorporate the changes from the repository with your changes; it won't just overwrite or throw away all your hard work!

During the update process, Subversion will let you know what's being changed in your working copy. It will show files that have been added or removed, files that have been updated, and files whose new contents have been merged with your local changes.

TortoiseSVN includes a "Show log..." button once the update completes, allowing you to easily see the log messages for recent changes. This can be especially useful if the update has caused a conflict.

Cornerstone is fairly quiet during an update. There is a small activity indicator at the bottom left of the window that shows an update is in progress. To see everything that Cornerstone has done recently, click the Transcript button on the bottom toolbar.

▶ Update your working copy to the latest revision.

```
prompt> cd ~/work/mbench
prompt> svn update
```

▶ Update your working copy using Tortoise.

Right-click the base directory in your working copy, and choose SVN Update. Tortoise will open a status window and update your working copy.

▶ Update your working copy using Cornerstone.

Select your project in the working copy sources list, and then click Update on the toolbar.

Related Tasks

- Task 18, *Handling Conflicts*, on the following page
- Task 21, *Viewing the Log*, on page 62

18 | Handling Conflicts

When two people change the same part of the same file, Subversion cannot automatically merge the changes. Conflicts are actually quite rare because they indicate that two people were working on exactly the same thing. Sometimes two developers will try to fix the same bug and end up changing the same file and cause a conflict or will be working on a common data structure and both change it. Being on the receiving end of a merge conflict is usually an indicator that you should be talking more often with your colleagues.

If Alice and Bob are both working on the same part of the same file and Alice checks in first, she won't notice a problem. When Bob comes to check in, he'll be told that his version of the file is out-of-date; he needs to do an update before he can commit. When he updates, Subversion will try to merge his changes with Alice's changes. Since both sets of changes are in the same part of the file, Subversion tells Bob that there is a *conflict*.

The Subversion command-line client provides various options for resolving conflicts. For each conflicted file, Subversion asks you to choose from the following commands:

p   Postpone fixing the conflict, and save the file with embedded conflict markers. You can find the conflicts by looking for sequences of < < < and > > > characters. Pick the text you'd like (your version, indicated by the text .mine; the version from the repository, indicated by a revision number; or a combination of the two), and then save the file.

df   Show a full diff of all the changes to the merged file. This shows all your changes to the file plus any conflict markers that would be inserted to show conflicts.

e   Edit the merged file using an editor. The file will contain conflict markers so you can find the conflicts and resolve them.

r   Mark the conflict as resolved, accepting any edits you have made.

mf   "My file"—ignore the changes from the repository, and use your version of the file in full.

tf   "Their file"—ignore your changes, and use the version of the file from the repository in full.

l   Launch an external merge tool[9] to merge the changes.

---

9. Use the environment variable SVN_MERGE to tell Subversion which merge tool you'd like to use.

▶ Use the command-line Subversion client to update and merge files.

During an svn update, Subversion could discover conflicting changes and need your help to resolve the conflict.

```
prompt> svn update
Conflict discovered in 'src/mbench.java'.
Select: (p) postpone, (df) diff-full, (e) edit,
        (h) help for more options:
```

Enter commands (detailed on the opposite page) to merge the conflicting changes. You can keep editing the files until you are happy.

▶ Mark conflicts as resolved.

For each file that was conflicted, use svn resolved to tell Subversion that you've fixed the problem.

```
prompt> svn resolved src/mbench.java
```

Related Tasks

- Task 8, *Seeing What You've Changed*, on page 26
- Task 17, *Updating to the Latest Revision*, on page 50
- Task 19, *Handling Conflicts Using Tortoise*, on the following page
- Task 20, *Handling Conflicts Using Cornerstone*, on page 56

19 Handling Conflicts Using Tortoise

During an update, Tortoise will keep track of any files that have conflicting changes, coloring them red in the update window. At the very end of the update log will be a message reminding you that some files were conflicted and that you should fix the problem. You can fix conflicts later by right-clicking files in Windows Explorer and choosing TortoiseSVN > Edit conflicts, but it's usually easiest to do it from the update window by double-clicking each conflicted file.

The TortoiseMerge window is split into three sections. The top-left pane shows "their" changes, that is, the changes someone else made and committed to the repository. The top-right pane shows "my" changes, that is, the changes we made in our working copy. The bottom pane shows the result from the merge.

In the example screenshot, we can see that both sets of changes have added diagnostic output when the mBench worker finishes testing Mongo. In the repository version, the source code shows the exact number of reads and writes performed. In our version, we simply state that the test is complete. Subversion doesn't know which block of code is correct, so TortoiseMerge shows a block of ??? characters as the merge result. We might decide the repository version is the correct one; right-click the block in the top-left pane, and choose "Use this text block." TortoiseMerge updates the output pane to show the result as you select blocks from the two conflicting change sets.

Use the red up and down arrows toward the top of the TortoiseMerge window to quickly move to the next (or previous) conflict. Once you have resolved all the conflicts, click the green tick icon on the menu bar to mark the file resolved.

▶ Update from the repository where there is a conflict.

Right-click the base directory in your working copy, and choose SVN Update. If there is a conflict, Tortoise will show conflicted files in red and warn you that there was a conflict.

▶ Use the TortoiseMerge tool to resolve conflicts.

For each conflicted file, double-click it to launch TortoiseMerge.

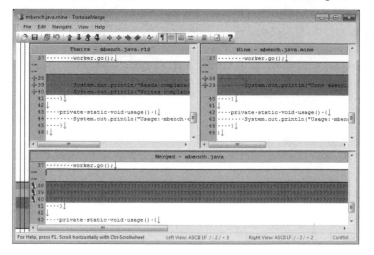

Related Tasks

- Task 8, *Seeing What You've Changed*, on page 26
- Task 17, *Updating to the Latest Revision*, on page 50
- Task 18, *Handling Conflicts*, on page 52

20 Handling Conflicts Using Cornerstone

When you update from the repository, Cornerstone will track any files where Subversion encounters a conflict. Unfortunately, Cornerstone is not very verbose in telling you that files are conflicted; you need to select the Modified or Conflicted view in the working copy browser in order to easily see conflicted files.

Cornerstone includes simple conflict resolution strategies. In most cases, you should edit the conflicted file to remove the <<< and >>> conflict markers. These markers are labeled so that you can see the difference between your version of the file and the repository version. For each conflict, determine what the correct code block should be, and edit the file to reflect your choice. Once you are satisfied that the conflicts are resolved, use the Resolved button to mark the file resolved.

In some cases, you will know that all conflicts in a file should be resolved by using the repository changes or by using your working copy changes. In this case, select the file in the working copy browser, and then click and hold the Resolve button on the bottom toolbar. Choose Resolve to Latest in Repository to have repository changes chosen in favor of your local changes. Choose Resolve to My Changes to have local changes chosen in favor of repository changes.

▶ Update from the repository where there is a conflict.

Select your project from the working copy sources list, and click Update on the toolbar. Click Changed to show just files that have changed and might have a conflict. If any of your files have a red C icon next to them, you have a conflict.

▶ Edit the file to resolve conflicts.

Double-click the conflicted file to launch the default editor for that file. Edit the file to remove Subversion's conflict markers.

▶ Mark the conflict as resolved.

Select the conflicted file using the working copy browser. Click the Resolved button on the bottom toolbar to mark the conflict resolved.

Related Tasks

• Task 8, *Seeing What You've Changed*, on page 26
• Task 17, *Updating to the Latest Revision*, on page 50
• Task 18, *Handling Conflicts*, on page 52

Part IV

Using the History

Version control tools like Subversion allow you to do more than simply keep your files in a safe place and collaborate with your team. Subversion stores every revision of every file that was ever committed to the repository. You can think of this detailed history as a kind of time machine—you can go back to any point in history if something goes wrong.

More than just being able to go back to a specific point in time and do things differently, Subversion's powerful history functions let you understand how things got to be the way they are today. Often you'll need to do some detective work to figure out why or when a certain bug was introduced, who last made a particular change, or which people were involved in developing certain functionality.

Subversion's history functions all depend on a key piece of information: the log messages associated with each revision. It's all too easy to leave the message blank or type something simple like "fixed a bug," but using a good log message will make things much easier for others doing detective work later.

Subversion already stores the textual changes that were made, so there's not much point writing a message that says "added BP network protocol." Instead, you should use the log message to indicate *why* you made the change:

Network connections to our Mars rover won't work using regular TCP networking because, even at the speed of light, signals can take twenty minutes to reach the rover. Bundle Protocol solves this problem by allowing much higher-latency network connections.

If the change being made is fixing a bug, you should include the bug identifier (number, code name) in the commit message. The other information about the bug—description, how to reproduce, and so on—doesn't need to be repeated.

Covered in this part:

- Browsing recent repository activity is covered in Task 21, *Viewing the Log*, on the following page.
- Examining exactly how a portion of a file got to its current state is covered in Task 22, *Detective Work with svn blame*, on page 64.
- Sometimes you'll want to undo a change that has already been committed to the repository. Task 23, *Reverting a Committed Revision*, on page 66 shows how to do this.

Let's start by looking at recent repository history.

21 Viewing the Log

When you are working as part of a project team, many people will be making changes and committing them to the repository. Depending on the size of your team and how often they commit, there might be dozens of changes every day. If you have been away from the project for a while, or even as part of your daily routine, you might want to check what has been committed recently.

Subversion's log stores every change ever committed to the repository. To see recent changes, you can ask Subversion to show the log for your working copy. Subversion shows changes in reverse chronological order, starting with the most recent change and then working backward. This might be a long list of changes—for the command-line client you should pipe the output into a pager program such as less. The graphical clients usually show just the last 100 or so changes unless you specifically ask for more.

Subversion will show log entries only for revisions that have been applied to your working copy. If you haven't updated your working copy for a while and ask to see the log, you won't see any recent changes that have been made by other people. To see those log messages, you'll need to update your working copy first.

Both Tortoise and Cornerstone provide easy ways to browse the log and examine changes in detail. You can scroll through the various log messages looking for something interesting and then click individual changed files and show the exact differences when that revision was committed. The first time you show the log, Cornerstone will offer to cache the log to speed up future requests. You should allow it to do so if you have a fairly fast connection to your Subversion server.

You can also show the log for a repository URL instead of a working copy. The command-line client works as follows:

```
prompt> svn log http://svn.mycompany.com/mbench/trunk
```

To show the log for a repository URL using TortoiseSVN, start the Repo Browser, and enter the URL for your repository. Right-click the base directory for your project, and choose Show Log.

To show the log for a repository using Cornerstone, select a repository from the repository source list, and then click the Log button to show the log.

► Show log entries for your working copy.

```
prompt> cd ~/work/myproject
prompt> svn log | less
```

► Show the log using Tortoise.

Right-click at the base of your working copy, and choose TortoiseSVN > Show Log. Select any log entry to see all the files that were changed, and double-click any file to show the diff for that file.

► Show the log using Cornerstone.

Select your project from the working copy sources list, and then click the Log button on the bottom toolbar. Cornerstone will show a list of revisions including their log message and when the change was made. Click the expander triangle next to Changes to show the full list of files that were changed, and double-click any file to show the diff for that file.

Related Tasks

- Task 22, *Detective Work with svn blame*, on the next page
- Task 23, *Reverting a Committed Revision*, on page 66

22 Detective Work with svn blame

While working on a programming task, it's often very useful to find out who most recently changed a particular piece of code. You might find the code hard to understand or have questions about it, or it might just be plain bad code, and you'd like to offer some advice to whoever wrote it.

The Subversion blame command tells you who is responsible for each line in a particular file. You can also use praise, annotate, and ann as synonyms for blame.

When you run the blame command, Subversion goes back through the history of the file and determines who most recently changed each line and when they changed it. In the command-line example on the facing page, we can see that mbench.java has two people who have changed it most recently, mike and tim. The numbers that Subversion prints by each line aren't line numbers; they are the revision in which that line was most recently changed.

Subversion is telling us who changed each line in the file and when that change was made. This *isn't* quite the same as telling us who wrote the code—if someone commits a change that adds something to a line, removes something, or even just changes whitespace, blame will put their name on that line of code. This is a subtle distinction, but blame is still useful because if someone is committing a change to a line of code, they should know what that code does.

TortoiseSVN shows the blame information in a scrollable window with usernames and revision numbers down the left side. Hover the mouse over a particular revision number to see extra information, including the log message for that revision. Right-clicking a revision number will give extra options, such as viewing the revision in full, including all the files that were changed.

As of this writing, Cornerstone unfortunately does not support showing blame information, so you'll need to use the command-line client instead.

▶ Show blame information using the command-line client.

```
mbench> svn blame src/mbench.java
11    mike import com.mongodb.Mongo;
  :     :       :
 6    mike public class mbench {
11    mike    public static void main(String[] args) {
11    mike       if (args.length != 3) {
 6    mike          usage();
 7    mike          return;
 6    mike       }
  :     :       :
11    mike       worker worker = new worker(db, runTime);
11    mike       worker.go();
12    mike
14     ian       long readsPerSec = worker.getReads() / runTime;
14     ian       long writesPerSec = worker.getWrites() / runTime;
14     ian       System.out.println("Reads/sec:  " + readsPerSec);
14     ian       System.out.println("Writes/sec: " + writesPerSec);
 6    mike    }
```

▶ Show blame information using Tortoise.

Navigate to your working copy using Windows Explorer. Right-click a file, and choose TortoiseSVN > Blame.... Click OK to use the default settings. TortoiseSVN will show blame information from the earliest revision of the file.

Related Tasks

- Task 8, *Seeing What You've Changed*, on page 26
- Task 21, *Viewing the Log*, on page 62

23 Reverting a Committed Revision

Sometimes you will want to undo a change that has been committed to the repository. You might find out that a change intended to fix a bug actually introduced a new bug, and you want to undo your attempted bug fix. The requirements for your software might have changed, meaning that some code changes you committed are no longer worthwhile. Whatever the reason, Subversion's history tracking tools allow you to go back and undo the changes that were made.

Subversion doesn't actually allow us to delete history from the repository; we can only keep moving forward. To undo an old revision, we have to reverse whatever changes were made in the old revision and then commit a new revision. This is called a *reverse merge*.

Use Subversion's history features to determine the change you want to revert. A reverse merge will update your *working copy* files so they no longer contain the changes from the original revision—you are not changing anything inside the repository so you will get a chance to test that the revert has worked properly. As with any merge operation, you might encounter conflicts. Task 18, *Handling Conflicts*, on page 52 has more information on dealing with conflicts.

If you only want to undo *part* of a committed revision rather than the *whole* revision, you need to revert some of your working copy files after Subversion has finished the reverse merge. For these files, you are reverting the reverse merge, which gets you back where you started.

If you want to revert only changes to a particular directory, then things are much easier. For the command-line client, change to the directory you want to revert before running the revert command. If you're using Tortoise, right-click the folder containing files you want to revert before using the log to find, and revert the change.

The change you are reverting might be recent, but it could also be quite old. Depending on how fast your code base evolves, other parts of the code may have changed since the original change was committed. You should always run a build before checking in to make sure that everything still works.

If you are reverting using Cornerstone, be aware that it works slightly differently than the command line and Tortoise clients. Reverting to a particular revision undoes *all* the changes made since that revision. In most cases this is still useful, but it's a little less surgical than doing a command-line reverse merge.

► Revert a revision using the command-line client.

```
mbench> svn merge -r 14:13 .
--- Reverse-merging r14 into '.':
G    .idea/workspace.xml
U    src/mbench.java
prompt> svn commit -m "Reverted revision 14"
```

► Revert a revision using Tortoise.

Browse to your working copy folder using Windows Explorer. Right-click the root folder, and choose TortoiseSVN > Show Log. Find the change you want to revert, and then right-click it and choose "Revert changes from this revision." Tortoise will reverse merge the change.

Run a build to make sure you haven't broken anything, and then commit your changes back into the repository.

► Revert a revision using Cornerstone.

In the working copy browser, select the items you want to revert to a previous revision, and then select Working Copy > Revert... from the Cornerstone menu.

Type a revision number or use the revision picker to choose the revision to which you want to revert. Click Revert to set the items back to the selected revision.

Run a build to make sure you haven't broken anything, and then commit your changes back into the repository.

Related Tasks

- Task 15, *Reverting Working Copy Changes*, on page 40
- Task 21, *Viewing the Log*, on page 62
- Task 18, *Handling Conflicts*, on page 52

Part V

Branching, Merging, and Tagging

Real-world software projects are rarely straightforward and easy. The team must develop the software, stabilize it ready to be released into production, and support it once it's in production. We've shown how a team can use Subversion to collaborate during development; this chapter will focus on how a team can release and support their software.

Usually when a team is preparing to release their software, they want to focus on quality. The team might decide to fix bugs and improve performance rather than adding new features. Generally, though, the team will want to continue some forward momentum. Maybe the team will split, with some developers working on stabilizing the code for release and everyone else developing as normal.

These two activities, stabilization and adding new features, generally cannot be done in the same code base. It's very likely that the new features will add instability to the software, which is exactly what we don't want when we're trying to put a release into production. The solution is to *branch* the code. Branching splits off a new line of development where stabilization and bug fixing can be done, while new features can continue to be added on the trunk. The following diagram shows the branch and the trunk visually:

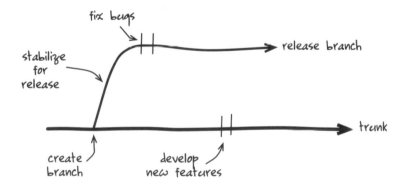

The first step is to create a branch. Branches are identified with a name and are stored in the branches directory within the Subversion repository. A branch starts out as an exact copy of the trunk but can be modified independently. One team can work on the branch, fixing bugs and stabilizing the code. Another team can work on the trunk, adding new features. The two teams will never accidentally surprise each other because they are working on different branches.

When working on a release branch, there are usually some bug fixes or other improvements that we'd like to include in the trunk. Rather than making a fix on the branch and then reimplementing the fix on the trunk, Subversion allows us to *merge* the change from the branch to the trunk. Subversion can do this because a branch is much more than a simple copy of the files. Subversion remembers the origin of the files on the trunk and the branch, and it uses their shared ancestry to make merges easier and more automatic. The dotted lines on the following diagram show changes being merged from the release branch to the trunk:

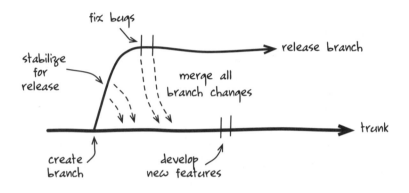

The diagram shows a fairly standard release branch strategy but does require a lot of merging because every change made on the branch needs to be merged back to the trunk. It's usually best to reduce the number of merges in your branching strategy because this reduces effort and the potential for a "forgotten" merge. We can change the branching strategy to reduce merging as follows. Stabilize for release *before* creating the branch, and then fix any bugs on the trunk and merge them to the branch. The branch diagram looks like this:

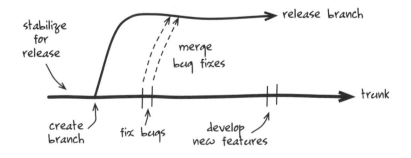

You might already be familiar with branching and merging and have your own strategy. This is fine; just make sure everyone on the team understands where they need to make fixes and where they should merge. If you're not careful and disciplined, it's possible to "lose" a change. For example, if you fixed a bug on the release branch but forgot to merge the fix to the trunk, the trunk still has that bug. The QA team might see the bug in a later release and call it a *regression* since from their perspective it was fixed once already.

Another strategy worth mentioning is called *feature branching*. A team might use this when a new feature will take a long time or cause some instability in the code base. Instead of developing the feature on the trunk, the team can create a branch specifically for the feature. The rest of development continues on the trunk as normal. The feature branch should be updated with trunk changes frequently—usually daily—to keep the feature branch "close" to the trunk. This merge from the trunk to the feature branch is known as *rebasing*. Once the feature is finished, merge the feature branch back to the trunk.

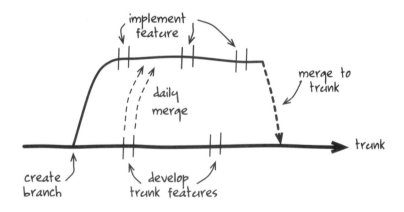

When a customer calls up with a problem, it's important to know exactly what code they are running so you can diagnose and fix the problem. You should only ship software to a customer from a release branch, but since the code on the branch can change over time, you need a better way to uniquely identify a release. With Subversion, you can *tag* the code that was used to build a release, giving it a number such as 2.0.3. To create a tag, you will copy your release branch into a named directory within the repository tags directory. Usually the tag name is also compiled into the software as a version number. Once you know what version your customer is running, you can check out the tagged code and get exactly the code that is running in production.

The following diagram shows a release branch with two tags, R-1.0.0 and R-1.0.1:

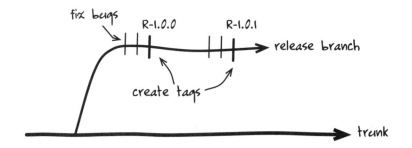

Covered in this part:

- Task 24, *Creating a Branch*, on page 76 shows how to create a release branch.

- If you have a trunk working copy and want to quickly switch to a branch, follow the instructions in Task 25, *Switching to a Branch*, on page 78.

- Task 26, *Merging Changes from Trunk to Branch*, on page 80 covers the process for merging changes, such as bug fixes, to a branch.

- Repeated merging, usually used to keep the trunk and a branch in sync, is discussed in Task 27, *Using Change Tracking*, on page 82.

- Tagging is explained in detail in Task 28, *Tagging a Release*, on page 84.

Let's start by creating a release branch.

24 Creating a Branch

Subversion branches are copies of the trunk and are stored in the branches directory inside the repository. The branches directory sits alongside the trunk directory, as we saw in Task 5, *Creating an Empty Project*, on page 14. This directory organization is a Subversion convention—nothing forces you to organize your repository in this way, but if you stick to the convention, it makes it easier for people to work with your project.

To create a branch, use the Subversion copy command to copy the trunk to a new location. You should always use repository URLs when creating a branch. You *can* copy the file revisions in a working copy to create a branch, but using a repository URL is much faster. It's also safer because if your working copy contains mixed revisions (not all the files in a working copy have to be at the same revision), Subversion will faithfully copy the mixed revisions to the branch, which usually isn't what you want to do.

Branches can be named using any characters that Subversion allows in a directory name, including spaces and characters with accents (although we suggest sticking to alphanumerics). Use a naming scheme that makes it easy to identify branches. Here we're using "RB" to indicate a release branch, followed by the version number of the branch. You could also organize your branches into different directories, such as releases/1.0.

Once you have created your branch, you can check out a working copy of the code. Make sure that you use a working copy directory name that makes it easy to identify the branch. In our example, we already have an mbench directory for the trunk working copy, so we check out into an mbench-1.0 directory for the 1.0 release branch.

► Create a release branch.

```
prompt> svn copy -m "Create 1.0 release branch" \
            http://svn.mycompany.com/mbench/trunk \
            http://svn.mycompany.com/mbench/branches/RB_1.0
```

► Check out the branch to a new working copy.

```
prompt> cd ~/work
prompt> svn checkout   \
            http://svn.mycompany.com/mbench/branches/RB_1.0  \
            mbench-1.0
```

► Create a branch using Tortoise.

Using Windows Explorer, right-click the base directory for your working copy, and choose TortoiseSVN > Branch/tag....

Edit the To URL setting, replacing trunk with branches/RB_1.0, and click OK.

Enter a log message, and click OK to create the branch.

► Create a branch using Cornerstone.

Select your repository from the repository source list, and then navigate to the trunk directory for your project.

Drag the trunk directory to the branches directory while holding down the Option key. Your mouse pointer will indicate you are about to make a copy with a green + icon.

Give the branch a name, click Copy, and then enter a log message. Click Continue to create the branch.

Related Tasks

- Task 7, *Checking Out a Working Copy*, on page 24
- Task 25, *Switching to a Branch*, on the following page
- Task 26, *Merging Changes from Trunk to Branch*, on page 80

25 Switching to a Branch

Once you have created a branch, changes made on the trunk will be isolated from changes made on the branch. To make changes to the branch, you need to have a working copy that is pointing at the branch instead of the trunk.

The easiest way to get a working copy of the branch is to check out a new working copy using the branch URL instead of the usual trunk URL. This leaves you with two working copies on your computer: one for the trunk and one for the branch. Sometimes it's not desirable to have two working copies, for example when the working copy is large and takes a long time to check out or when you have application servers or databases configured to point to the working copy.

The switch command tells Subversion to take an existing working copy and update it so that it is pointing at a different branch. Subversion figures out what version of the files you have in your working copy and then merges changes as necessary to reflect the state of the branch. A switched working copy, under most circumstances, is identical to a freshly checked-out copy of the branch.

If you spend a lot of time switching between branches, it's possible to lose track of where a particular working copy is pointing. The svn info command will print out this information. If you're using Tortoise, right-clicking in any working copy folder and choosing TortoiseSVN > Repo-browser will always pop up the browser pointing to wherever your working copy is pointed.

Sometimes you might do some work in a working copy, such as fixing a bug, and then realize that you should have done the work on a branch instead. Your work is not wasted, however. Switching to a branch attempts to leave your working copy changes intact, so you can switch your working copy to the branch and then check in your changes.

It's very easy to lose track of where you are if you switch a working copy a lot. We recommend using multiple working copies for each of your branches and avoiding switching where possible.

Cornerstone does not include an option to switch a working copy. Use multiple working copies for each of your branches instead.

► Switch to a branch.

```
prompt> cd work/mbench
mbench> svn switch http://svn.mycompany.com/mbench/branches/RB_1.0
```

► Switch to a branch using Tortoise.

Using Windows Explorer, navigate to the base directory for your working copy. Right-click the base directory, and choose TortoiseSVN > Switch....

Edit the To URL setting to reflect the branch you'd like to switch to, or press the ... button to use the repo browser to find the branch.

Click OK to perform the switch.

Related Tasks

- Task 24, *Creating a Branch*, on page 76
- Task 26, *Merging Changes from Trunk to Branch*, on the next page

26 Merging Changes from Trunk to Branch

When stabilizing your code ready for release, it's best to fix bugs on the trunk and then merge the fixes to the branch. If you do things the other way around, you might forget to merge a fix back to the trunk, and it will show up as a regression in your next release.

Fix the bug on the trunk, and note the revision number where the fix was checked in. In a branch working copy, merge the revision or revisions from the trunk. In most cases, the merge will work automatically without any conflicts. The merge works kind of like an update; think of the branch as an old working copy that needs to incorporate new changes from the trunk to keep it up-to-date. If the trunk and the branch have diverged, though, merging the change might create a conflict. See Task 18, *Handling Conflicts*, on page 52 for more information about resolving conflicts.

After merging the changes, you should run a build to make sure that you haven't broken anything. You should also check to ensure the fix is still working and that the bug is no longer present on the branch version of the code. Check in the changes to complete the merge.

When checking in, it's a good idea to use a log message that includes the revisions you merged and the number or identifier for the bug that you're fixing. The other members of your team will thank you for the extra information if they have to chase down a bug fix later.

Tortoise includes some nice GUI tools for finding and merging revisions, so you don't need to do quite as much work remembering revision numbers. Cornerstone unfortunately does not include merge functionality, so you'll need to use the command-line client for Mac merging.

► Merge a single revision to a branch.

```
prompt> cd work/mbench-1.0
mbench-1.0> svn merge -c 16 http://svn.mycompany.com/mbench/trunk
mbench-1.0> svn commit -m "Merged r16 (fix bug-7) from the trunk"
```

► Merge a range of revisions to a branch.

```
prompt> cd work/mbench-1.0
mbench-1.0> svn merge -r 19:22 http://svn.mycompany.com/mbench/trunk
mbench-1.0> svn commit -m \
            "Merged r19-22 from the trunk (fix bugs 9 and 11)"
```

► Merge revisions using Tortoise.

Right-click in the base directory of a branch working copy, and choose TortoiseSVN > Merge....

Select "Merge a range of revisions" as the merge type, and click Next.

Enter the URL for the project trunk in the "URL to merge from" box. Alternatively, click the ... button and use the repo browser to find the trunk.

Enter revision numbers to merge, or press the "Show log" button to choose revisions based on their log message.

Click Next to go to the Merge options screen, leave all the settings at their defaults, and click Merge to complete the merge.

Check in your changes using a log message that includes a list of the revisions you merged.

Related Tasks

- Task 24, *Creating a Branch*, on page 76
- Task 25, *Switching to a Branch*, on page 78

27 Using Change Tracking

Sometimes a team will use a *feature branch* to work on a major change that might be disruptive to developers working on the trunk. The work can proceed safely on the branch, and when completed, the changes are merged to the trunk, and the branch is deleted.

A feature might take a while to complete, increasing the risk that the trunk and the feature branch diverge and making the impending "merge to trunk" more difficult. Developers working on the branch might choose to periodically pull changes from the trunk to the feature branch in order to reduce this risk, a technique known as *rebasing*. Subversion's merge tracking feature allows us to automatically merge any trunk changes to a branch that have not previously been merged and to repeat this merge as often as we'd like.

In the example on the facing page, we would like to add internationalization to our software in the DEV_i18n branch. We start with the feature branch already created and two working copies, mbench for the trunk and mbench_i18n for the feature branch. Internationalization might take a while, so we periodically *reintegrate* changes from the trunk. Run the reintegration frequently, at least once a week. Each time Subversion will only pick up new changes from the trunk that haven't yet been merged to the branch.

Once the work on the feature branch is complete, merge from the feature branch to the trunk. Subversion will only merge changes that were made on the feature branch; it won't try to merge changes that originally came from the trunk. Because we have used merge tracking to keep the trunk and the branch close together, merging the feature branch to the trunk should be straightforward.

Merge tracking requires Subversion 1.6 or newer.[10] If you are using an older release of Subversion, you can achieve the same effect of keeping the branch and the trunk close together, but you'll need to manually track which changes have been merged and do all your merges explicitly. There are certain situations that merge tracking cannot handle, such as file renames and deletes. If your team does a lot of refactoring, you should ask people to avoid doing renames or deletes while you are working on a feature branch.

---

10. Change tracking was first implemented in Subversion 1.5, but the newer 1.6 release includes substantial improvements and bug fixes. You really should use Subversion 1.6 or newer if you want change tracking.

▶ Merge outstanding changes from the trunk to a feature branch.

```
prompt> cd work/mbench_i18n
mbench_18n> svn update
mbench_18n> svn merge --reintegrate \
            http://svn.mycompany.com/mbench/trunk
mbench_18n> svn commit -m "Merged all pending trunk changes"
```

▶ Merge a completed feature branch to the trunk.

```
prompt> cd work/mbench
mbench> svn update
mbench> svn merge --reintegrate \
        http://svn.mycompany.com/mbench/branches/DEV_i18n
mbench> svn commit -m "Merged feature branch DEV_i18n"
```

▶ Merge trunk changes to a feature branch using Tortoise.

Right-click the base directory of your branch working copy, and choose TortoiseSVN > Merge....

Select "Reintegrate a branch" as the merge type, and click Next.

Enter the URL for the project trunk in the "from URL" box.

Click Next to go to the Merge options screen, leave all the settings at their defaults, and click Merge to complete the merge.

▶ Merge a completed feature branch using Tortoise.

Right-click the base directory of your trunk working copy, and choose TortoiseSVN > Merge....

Select "Reintegrate a branch" as the merge type, and click Next.

Enter the URL for the feature branch in the "from URL" box.

Click Next to go to the Merge options screen, leave all the settings at their defaults, and click Merge to complete the merge.

Related Tasks

- Task 24, *Creating a Branch*, on page 76
- Task 25, *Switching to a Branch*, on page 78
- Task 26, *Merging Changes from Trunk to Branch*, on page 80

28 Tagging a Release

When creating a build of your software, especially one that will be released to a customer, it's important to know exactly what source code was used. We can use a Subversion *tag* to record which revisions of files were used in a build.

As part of the release process, someone needs to compile the software. Usually this is a manual process done by one of the developers, but it can also be automated. You might have a build box that automatically builds your software every time a developer makes a change. Either way, you should have a process for building the software and assigning it a build number.

Use the Subversion copy command to copy your working copy to a new directory in your project's tags directory. You should create a tag from the working copy that was used to make the build, rather than the repository HEAD revision, because other changes could have been checked in since you started the build. Creating a tag from your working copy guarantees that the tag contains exactly the revisions of the files that were used to make the build. If your release is being created by an automated build server, it will still have a working copy that it uses to compile the code. The build server should create a tag from this working copy as part of the build process.

Cornerstone does not allow creation of a tag from a working copy, so you'll need to be a little bit more careful when tagging releases. Use the log browser to update your working copy to a particular revision, run your build, and then use the same revision when creating the tag.

You might have noticed that creating a tag and creating a branch both create a copy of the files within the repository. This means that, in theory at least, you could commit changes to a tag. A tag that has changed wouldn't be much use for identifying which files went into a build, so by convention tags are *read-only*. Developers should never commit changes to a tag, and this can be enforced by using a hook script in your repository. Task 42, *Using Repository Hooks*, on page 124 includes an example of how to make your tags directories read-only.

▶ Create a release tag from a working copy.

```
prompt> cd work/mbench-1.0
mbench-1.0> svn update
mbench-1.0> svn copy . \
            http://svn.mycompany.com/mbench/tags/REL_1.0.0 \
            -m "Create R1.0.0 tag"
```

▶ Create a release tag using Tortoise.

Right-click the base directory of your working copy, and choose TortoiseSVN > Branch/tag....

Click the ... button, and use the repo browser to navigate to your project's tags directory. Click OK, and then edit the URL so that it ends with the desired tag name, for example tags/REL_1.0.0.

Pick which revision you'd like to create the tag from, usually either from a specific revision or from your working copy.

Enter a log message, and click OK to create the tag.

▶ Create a release tag using Cornerstone.

Select your repository from the repository source list. Use the repository browser to find your release branch. Opt+drag the branch folder to the tags folder (the cursor will change to a green + icon to indicate the copy), and then release the mouse button.

Enter a name for the new tag such as REL_1.0.0. Click Copy, write a short log message, and then click Continue to create the tag.

Related Tasks

- Task 7, *Checking Out a Working Copy*, on page 24
- Task 24, *Creating a Branch*, on page 76

Part VI

File Locking

Subversion enables a team to collaborate on a project by sharing their files in the central repository. Everyone on the team is allowed to edit any file in their working copy, and if two people edit the same file at the same time, Subversion helps you merge the two edits later. This is effectively an *optimistic locking* scheme. Subversion knows that most of the time two people won't be editing the same file, so it allows things to proceed and provides tools to fix the occasional collision when it occurs.

If you're coming from a different version control tool, you might be used to *pessimistic locking*. This is a scheme where if you want to change a file, you first have to lock the file for editing. Once you are done making changes, you can commit the changes and release the lock. Pessimistic locking avoids the need to merge two people's edits but at a huge cost—only one person can work on a file at any particular time. For a development team, this is a disaster. The team can spend all day negotiating with each other about who is going to lock a file and asking "Are you done yet?" It can be particularly grating when someone locks a file and then goes home early—the rest of the team is stalled until they get back.

Subversion's "copy, modify, merge" scheme allows development to flow more naturally, and its merge tools will usually automatically merge sets of changes. Merging works great for text-based files—source code, XML, SQL, and so on—but it won't work at all for binary files such as spreadsheets, word processing documents, pictures, and movies. For these kinds of files, you might want to use pessimistic locking to avoid merges.

Subversion's file locking features allow you to specify that certain files should be locked before they are edited. Subversion will check them out as read-only in the working copy. Most good editing tools will notice that a file is read-only, prompting the user to obtain a lock on the file before doing their work. The user can make edits to the file and then commit their changes, which also releases the lock. Subversion provides some features so that authorized users can break existing locks, which helps get around the "Joe locked a file and went on vacation" problem.

Covered in this part:

- Instructing Subversion to enforce file locking for a particular file is covered in Task 29, *Enabling File Locking*, on page 92.

- To make changes to a file where locking is enabled, you first need to lock the file for your use. Task 30, *Obtaining a Lock*, on page 94 shows you how to do this.

- Task 31, *Releasing a Lock*, on page 96 discusses how and when you should relinquish a lock.

- In some circumstances, you'll need to unlock a file that someone else has already locked. Task 32, *Breaking Someone Else's Lock*, on page 98 shows you how to do this and discusses when it's appropriate to do so.

Let's start by enabling file locking for specific files.

29 Enabling File Locking

Subversion file locking is supported on all files within the repository, so a user can in theory lock a file at any time. When someone else tries to commit a change to the locked file, Subversion will reject the change because the file is locked. This isn't very useful, though, because someone could have done a bunch of work that they now need to throw away because someone else has locked the file. A much better solution would be to stop a user from editing a file unless they have a lock on it in the first place.

Subversion's advisory locking is enabled by setting the special svn:needs-lock property on a file. It doesn't matter what value the property is set to; if the property is present, the file has locking enabled. Most teams set svn:needs-lock to something simple like * or yes.

Once you have set the property on any files that need locking, you need to commit the changes to the repository. After that point, anyone updating a working copy will find those files marked read-only on their computer. If a team member doesn't update their working copy for a while, they won't know about the new locking requirement on the files. For this reason, it's a good idea to enable file locking as soon as you add a nonmergeable file to the repository.

There is nothing forcing you to enable locking on all nonmergeable files in your repository. You might decide that small website graphics used primarily by your development team change so infrequently that it's not worth locking them. A spreadsheet containing critical reference data might be changed daily and be a much better candidate for locking. In general, try to keep file locking to a minimum. Locking imposes an overhead every time anyone wants to edit a file and is worth doing only if your team is regularly wasting effort on unmergeable changes.

To disable file locking on a particular file, just remove the svn:needs-lock property by using the svn propdel command. If you're using Tortoise, choose TortoiseSVN > Properties, and delete the property. If you're using Cornerstone, set Needs Lock back to No inside the file Inspector panel.

► Mark a file that needs locking.

```
mbench> svn propset svn:needs-lock yes docs/benchmarks.xlsx
mbench> svn commit -m "Spreadsheet requires a lock before editing"
```

► Mark a file that needs locking using Tortoise.

Using Windows Explorer, right-click the file, and choose TortoiseSVN > Properties.

Click the New... button, and then use the Property name drop-down to choose svn:needs-lock. Type any text you like into the property value, usually something like yes or true is best.

Click OK twice to save your changes to the file's properties, and then commit your changes to save the new property to the repository.

► Mark a file that needs locking using Cornerstone.

Select your project from the working copy sources list, and then expand the working copy browser until you find the file you want to lock.

Select the file, and click the Inspector icon on the Cornerstone toolbar. The Inspector panel will open on the right side of the Cornerstone window.

Select the Properties button within the Inspector panel, and set the Needs Lock drop-down to yes. Click Save Changes, and then press the Commit button on the toolbar to save your changes to the repository.

Related Tasks

- Task 30, *Obtaining a Lock*, on the next page
- Task 31, *Releasing a Lock*, on page 96
- Task 32, *Breaking Someone Else's Lock*, on page 98

30 | Obtaining a Lock

Files that are tagged with the special svn:needs-lock property are read-only in your working copy. How "read-only" is implemented depends on your operating system. On Windows, a file has a read-only attribute that you can see by right-clicking and choosing Properties. On a Unix system the file's write flag is disabled, and on a Mac the file will be set to read-only if you look in Finder's Sharing and Permissions section.

The Subversion client marks files read-only to give you a reminder that you should lock them before making changes. Depending on what software you use to edit the files, you may or may not get some kind of a prompt or warning indicating that the files are read-only. For example, using Paint on Windows to edit a graphics file, you'll be told the file is read-only only when you try to save it. Using Microsoft Excel to open a spreadsheet will put *[Read-Only]* in the window title to indicate the file is read-only but will still let you edit the spreadsheet. If you're going to use file locking, you should make sure that you understand how your editing tool will let you know the file is read-only.

When obtaining a lock, you can include a comment indicating why you've locked the file. This is useful if you are going to have the file locked for a while, because other users can query the repository to see your lock message.

If no one else has locked the file, your lock operation should succeed. Your Subversion client will mark the file read-write in your working copy.

The lock operation can fail if someone else has already locked the file. In this case, your Subversion client will tell you their username so you can go ask them when they will be done making their changes and maybe wait for them to unlock the file. In some cases, you might need to forcibly break or "steal" a lock; see Task 32, *Breaking Someone Else's Lock*, on page 98 for more information.

Locking a file will fail if your working copy is out-of-date. The command-line client and Tortoise will tell you what's wrong, with Tortoise even offering to update the file for you and try again. Unfortunately, Cornerstone will just quietly fail to lock the file; you won't get a little padlock icon indicating a lock. If locking fails, update your working copy and then try the lock again.

▶ Lock a file for editing.

```
docs> svn update
docs> svn lock benchmarks.xlsx -m "Adding 64-bit results"
'benchmarks.xlsx' locked by user 'mike'.
```

▶ Lock a file using Tortoise.

Using Windows Explorer, right-click the file you want to lock, and choose "SVN Get lock...."

Enter a message describing why you are locking the file, and then click OK to lock the file.

▶ Lock several files using Tortoise.

Using Windows Explorer, right-click the base directory of your working copy, and choose "TortoiseSVN > Get lock...."

Tortoise will display all the files in your working copy, along with a column indicating whether the files are marked as needing a lock.

Check the files you want to lock, enter a message describing why you are locking the files, and then click OK to lock the files.

▶ Lock a file using Cornerstone.

Using the working copy browser, find the file you want to lock. Files that need locks are indicated with a little tag icon just after the revision column in the browser.

Cmd+click the file, and choose Lock.... Provide a message indicating why you are locking the file, and then click Lock. A padlock icon will appear, signifying that you have locked the file.

Related Tasks

- Task 29, *Enabling File Locking*, on page 92
- Task 31, *Releasing a Lock*, on the following page
- Task 32, *Breaking Someone Else's Lock*, on page 98

31 Releasing a Lock

After locking a file, you might change your mind and decide not to modify it. Subversion releases all the locks in a working copy when you commit a change, but if you're not going to check in for a while, it would probably be polite to release the lock straightaway so someone else can lock the file if they need to do so.

Subversion will happily let you release a lock even if you have modified the locked file. If you later check in changes to the unlocked file, you have essentially avoided Subversion's locking mechanism. This is bad news. Someone else could edit the file in the meantime, and your commit could force them to redo their work. You should always revert changes to a file when you release a lock.

▶ Unlock a file.

```
docs> svn unlock benchmarks.xlsx
'benchmarks.xlsx' unlocked.
```

▶ Unlock a file using Tortoise.

Using Windows Explorer, right-click a locked file, and choose TortoiseSVN > Release lock.

Alternatively, right-click a working copy folder, and choose TortoiseSVN > Release lock. Tortoise will display all locked files within that directory.

Check the files you want to unlock, and then click OK.

▶ Unlock a file using Cornerstone.

Using the working copy browser, find the file you want to unlock. Locked files are indicated with a padlock icon.

Cmd+click the file, and choose Unlock.

Related Tasks

- Task 29, *Enabling File Locking*, on page 92
- Task 30, *Obtaining a Lock*, on page 94
- Task 32, *Breaking Someone Else's Lock*, on the following page

32 Breaking Someone Else's Lock

File locking is a consensual activity; it's designed to save a team effort where more than one person might change an unmergeable file. Sometimes, though, someone might not play by the rules. If a team member locks a file and goes home for the night (or worse goes on vacation!), then no one else is able to lock and edit the file. Subversion allows us to forcibly break a lock or more commonly to steal a lock from someone else.

Stealing a lock is usually preferred, because the Subversion server will unlock the file and relock it for a different user all in one atomic operation. If instead we unlock the file and then try to relock it, there's a small chance that another user can get in first and lock the file ahead of us. Once the file has been relocked or the lock stolen, the person with the new lock can continue as usual.

If you are the unfortunate user who went home for the night and had their lock stolen, things aren't so great. The Subversion client still sees a locked file in the working copy, but the lock is no longer valid. In Subversion terms, the lock is *defunct*. If you try to commit a change using the defunct lock, Subversion will refuse, and you'll have no choice but to revert your changes, lock the file again, and make the changes again.

The Subversion client notices defunct locks any time a working copy is updated from the repository, so it's good practice to update frequently. It would also be polite, should you break someone else's lock, to email them to let them know.

By default, Subversion allows any user to break or steal a lock. If you want to restrict this ability, Subversion's pre-lock and pre-unlock hook scripts can allow or prevent lock and unlock operations. The post-lock and post-unlock hook scripts can be used to perform additional processing such as sending an email when a lock is broken. Task 42, *Using Repository Hooks*, on page 124 covers hooks in more detail.

▶ Forcibly unlock a file.

```
docs> svn lock benchmarks.xlsx
svn: warning: Path '/trunk/docs/benchmarks.xlsx' is already locked
by user 'mmason' in filesystem '/home/svn/mbench/db'
docs> svn unlock --force benchmarks.xlsx
'benchmarks.xlsx' unlocked.
```

▶ Steal a lock.

```
docs> svn lock benchmarks.xlsx
svn: warning: Path '/trunk/docs/benchmarks.xlsx' is already locked
by user 'mmason' in filesystem '/home/svn/mbench/db'
docs> svn lock --force benchmarks.xlsx
'benchmarks.xlsx' locked by user 'mike'.
```

▶ Steal a lock using Tortoise.

Using Windows Explorer, navigate to the file for which you want to steal the lock, right-click, and choose "SVN Get lock...."

Enter an optional message describing why you are locking the file, and then check the "Steal the locks" option. Click OK to steal the locks.

▶ Steal a lock using Cornerstone.

In the Cornerstone menu, select the View menu, and ensure Show Repository Status is enabled. This instructs Cornerstone to query the repository looking for locks; files that are locked by someone else will be indicated with a gray padlock icon.

Select your project from the working copy sources list, and then expand the working copy browser to find the file for which you want to steal the lock. Cmd+click the file, and choose Lock... to attempt to lock the file.

Related Tasks

- Task 29, *Enabling File Locking*, on page 92
- Task 30, *Obtaining a Lock*, on page 94
- Task 31, *Releasing a Lock*, on page 96

Part VII

Setting Up a Server

Subversion stores your files inside a repository, which itself is just a collection of files on a disk somewhere. Subversion allows you to create an arbitrary directory structure inside the repository to organize your projects and files. Usually a repository will contain multiple projects, each inside their own directory. The top level of a repository like this will contain a directory for each project, and then each of the project directories will contain the usual trunk, tags, and branches directories. Alternatively, you might have a repository dedicated to each project. In this type of repository, the trunk, tags, and branches directories appear at the top level of the repository.

This might sound like a complicated choice, but don't worry. Unless you have a specific reason to separate projects into their own repositories, just set up a single repository and host multiple projects inside it. Once the repository is exposed using a URL, a user actually can't tell which hosting style is in use—this really is just an administrative decision.

To make a repository useful for a development team, we need to add a Subversion server so the files are available over a network. A variety of different servers are available for Subversion; you need to pick one that matches your needs.

svnserve is the simplest and easiest-to-use server. It's very lightweight and speaks a custom svn protocol. Unfortunately, svnserve doesn't provide encryption so is usually limited to LAN use where you have control of all the network traffic.

Secure Shell can be used to protect svnserve connections by adding a secure, encrypted SSH connection. This provides bulletproof security but at quite a high administrative cost since each Subversion user needs to have a corresponding Unix user account.

The Apache web server can be used to allow Subversion repository access using http and https connections, just like those used by a web browser. This is by far the most popular way to put a Subversion repository online. Using an SSL certificate, you get the same security used by websites to protect credit card information. You can also integrate with an existing user credentials store such as LDAP or even Active Directory. Using Apache makes it easy to serve multiple repositories from a single machine, and it allows you to apply fine-grained security to each repository, right down to the directory level.

This part of the book focuses on using Apache as a Subversion server on the Ubuntu Linux operating system, but we also show how to run a server on Windows using svnserve. We also include some recipes for backing up and restoring your repository and some tips on repository security.

Covered in this part:

- Task 33, *Installing Subversion Server*, on page 106 shows how to install Subversion on Ubuntu Linux.

- Once you have a Subversion server running, you need to create a repository that will be served up over the network. Task 34, *Creating a Repository*, on page 108 shows how to do this.

- Task 35, *Installing Subversion Server on Windows*, on page 110 covers using Windows as a Subversion server.

- Not everyone wants to run their own Subversion server. Task 36, *Using Third-Party Subversion Hosting*, on page 112 discusses how to use a third-party hosting service.

- If you have an existing CVS repository, you can convert it to a Subversion repository and keep all your history, branches, and tags. Task 37, *Migrating a CVS Repository*, on page 114 covers this in detail.

- Repository backup and subsequent restoration is covered in Task 38, *Backing Up and Restoring*, on page 116.

- Task 39, *Performing Full Weekly Backups*, on page 118 and Task 40, *Performing Incremental Daily Backups*, on page 120 together describe an efficient backup regime.

- You should never put an unsecured repository online. Task 41, *Securing a Repository*, on page 122 shows how to apply simple user- and group-based security to your repository.

- Task 42, *Using Repository Hooks*, on page 124 covers how to influence Subversion's revision commit life cycle so you can do interesting stuff such as blocking commits or sending post-commit emails.

Let's start by getting a Subversion server installed.

33 | Installing Subversion Server

Apache is by far the most popular method for getting a Subversion repository online. Most Linux servers come with Apache preinstalled, and at last count Apache runs more than half of all the servers on the Internet.[11] Using Apache makes your repository available via HTTP, and you can take advantage of all of Apache's other features such as SSL security, LDAP user authentication, and so on.

The Apache Subversion modules add extra directives that you can use in Apache configuration files. If you're hosting multiple websites on a single server, you can add a Subversion repository to a particular site by configuring its virtual host rather than using the global dav_syn.conf

In this example we're using the SVNParentPath directive so that every directory underneath /home/svn will be assumed to contain a repository. If you need a new repository, simply create one; you don't need to reconfigure Apache. If you instead use the SVNPath directive, you will host a single repository. Sometimes it's better to use just a single repository because it's less hassle to administer, back up, and so on. Even a single repository can host multiple projects, so both approaches can work.

If you use the configuration described here, a repository created in /home/svn/myrepo will be available on your Apache server at http://myserver.com/svn/myrepo.

When using htpasswd, you only need to use the -c argument when you first create the file. After that, drop the argument to add new users to an existing file. This isn't particularly intuitive, but htpasswd has been around a lot longer than Subversion and isn't quite as friendly. If you are using virtual hosts with Apache, you can use a different password file for each site. If you're using SVNPath, you can have a different password file for each repository.

Once you complete the configuration, you need to restart Apache. You can then create repositories, as described in Task 34, *Creating a Repository*, on page 108.

---

11. http://news.netcraft.com/archives/2010/06/16/june-2010-web-server-survey.html

▶ Install Apache and the Subversion modules.

```
prompt> sudo apt-get update
prompt> sudo apt-get install apache2 libapache2-svn
```

You can also use the Synaptic package manager to install the apache2 and libapache2-svn packages and any dependencies.

▶ Create a repositories directory.

```
prompt> sudo mkdir /home/svn
prompt> sudo chown www-data /home/svn
```

▶ Configure Apache to serve your Subversion repositories.

Edit /etc/apache2/mods-enabled/dav_svn.conf to configure Subversion. Your configuration should look like this:

```
<Location /svn>
  DAV svn

  SVNParentPath /home/svn

  AuthType Basic
  AuthName "Subversion Repository"
  AuthUserFile /home/svn/passwd

</Location>
```

▶ Create a Subversion password file.

```
prompt> sudo htpasswd -c /home/svn/passwd fred
prompt> sudo htpasswd /home/svn/passwd barney
prompt> sudo chown www-data /home/svn/passwd
```

▶ Restart Apache to apply your changes.

```
prompt> sudo service apache2 restart
```

Related Tasks

- Task 35, *Installing Subversion Server on Windows*, on page 110
- Task 5, *Creating an Empty Project*, on page 14
- Task 36, *Using Third-Party Subversion Hosting*, on page 112

34 | Creating a Repository

Subversion stores files inside a repository, which is simply a directory on the server that has been initialized using the svnadmin create command. If you are using Apache to host the Subversion server, as described in Task 33, *Installing Subversion Server*, on page 106, you also need to set the permissions on the directory so the www-user user can modify and create files in the directory.

If you're using the SVNParentPath directive, you're telling Apache that within a particular directory on your server, any *sub*directory is a Subversion repository, and Apache should make each repository available over the network. Most often with this style of configuration you're creating a separate repository for each project in which case you should name the directory after the project rather than calling it myrepos.

If you use the configuration described here, a repository created in /home/svn/myproject will be available on your Apache server at http://myserver.com/svn/myproject.

► Create a directory for the repository.

```
prompt> cd /home/svn
svn> sudo mkdir myrepos
```

► Initialize the new repository.

```
svn> sudo svnadmin create myrepos
svn> sudo chown -R www-data myrepos
```

Related Tasks

- Task 33, *Installing Subversion Server*, on page 106
- Task 5, *Creating an Empty Project*, on page 14
- Task 36, *Using Third-Party Subversion Hosting*, on page 112

35 Installing Subversion Server on Windows

CollabNet is the commercial sponsor for the Subversion project and builds a number of products using Subversion. They also offer training and support services, as well as a number of prebuilt binaries for Subversion. The instructions on the facing page allow you to install svnserve for Windows, but the CollabNet installer also allows you to install Apache. You might use Apache if you need more flexibility or to make a Subversion repository available over the Web.

The CollabNet configuration for svnserve ensures that any directory created inside C:\svn_repos is served as a repository. If you want to create multiple repositories, just create several directories, and use svnadmin create to initialize a repository in each directory.

Inside the repository Subversion stores configuration files in a conf directory. These are plain-text files, and you can edit them with any text editor.

The svnserve.conf file contains settings for access control, password files, and path-based access control. The file is well commented; read through and uncomment settings to configure svnserve to your liking.

Once you have configured svnserve, you need to use Control Panel to start the service. On Windows XP, you'll find this under Administrative Tools. For Windows Vista onward, you can just search for *services*. You only need to start the service manually once; the service will start automatically the next time the computer is rebooted.

Point a Subversion client at svn://localhost/repos to test that your installation has succeeded. If the client connection succeeds, you can start creating project directories within the repository, as described in Task 5, *Creating an Empty Project*, on page 14.

► Download and install CollabNet Subversion server.

Visit http://www.open.collab.net/downloads/subversion/, and download the Subversion "server and client" for Windows. Double-click the installer to start the installation process.

When the installer asks you to choose components, ensure svnserve is selected and Apache is not selected.

On the svnserve configuration screen, accept the default options. Make sure "install as Windows service" is selected, and then click Next a few times to complete the installation.

► Create a repository directory, and initialize the repository.

Click Start > Run..., and type cmd to start a command prompt. Enter the following commands:

```
C:\users\mmason> cd \svn_repository
C:\svn_repository> md repos
C:\svn_repository> svnadmin create repos
```

► Configure security for your repository.

Edit C:\svn_repository\repos\conf\svnserve.conf, and uncomment the password-db line to enable a password database. Save the file.

Edit C:\svn_repository\repos\conf\passwd. Enter users and passwords in the file as follows:

```
[users]
mike = s3cr3t
jim = b4n4n4
```

► Start svnserve using Windows Control Panel.

Scroll down until you find CollabNet Subversion svnserve. Select it, and then click the green "play" icon on the toolbar.

Related Tasks

• Task 5, *Creating an Empty Project*, on page 14
• Task 36, *Using Third-Party Subversion Hosting*, on the next page

36 Using Third-Party Subversion Hosting

If you don't want to run and maintain your own Subversion server, there are a number of third-party hosting services that will provide a server for you.

If you are developing open source software, SourceForge[12] will host your Subversion repository for free. Sign up on the website, and create your project. SourceForge will create a repository for your project, and you can begin using it. Remember to create the trunk, tags, and branches directories before starting work.

Commercial hosting is available if you want to keep your source code private. Many hosting providers are available, and they often include additional features such as bug trackers, wikis, and mailing lists. You can usually try these services for free, either for a certain trial period or with restrictions on the size of your repository or the number of developers. A free trial is a good way to check out a particular service provider.

Unfuddle[13] is one such provider, offering free trials with one project and a repository up to 200MB. After you've created your account, click the Repositories tab and then New Repository. As with SourceForge, remember to create trunk, tags, and branches directories before starting work.

Beanstalk[14] is another commercial hosting service that offers both Subversion and Git repositories. Their free account allows you to create one repository with up to three users and is limited to 100MB of storage.

---

12. http://www.sourceforge.net/
13. http://unfuddle.com/
14. http://beanstalkapp.com/

▶ Create a project on SourceForge.

Visit SourceForge, and create an account for yourself. Log in, and create a new project. Once active, you can check out from your project's new Subversion repository:

```
prompt> svn mkdir
        https://myproject.svn.sourceforge.net/svnroot/myproject/trunk
prompt> svn mkdir
        https://myproject.svn.sourceforge.net/svnroot/myproject/tags
prompt> svn mkdir
        https://myproject.svn.sourceforge.net/svnroot/myproject/branches
prompt> cd /home/work
work> svn checkout
        https://myproject.svn.sourceforge.net/svnroot/myproject/trunk
```

▶ Create a project using Unfuddle.

Visit Unfuddle, and create an account for yourself. Log in, and create a new trial project. You can check out from your project's new Subversion repository:

```
prompt> svn mkdir http://myuser.unfuddle.com/svn/myuser_myproject/trunk
prompt> svn mkdir http://myuser.unfuddle.com/svn/myuser_myproject/tags
prompt> svn mkdir http://myuser.unfuddle.com/svn/myuser_myproject/branches
prompt> cd /home/work
work> svn checkout http://myuser.unfuddle.com/svn/myuser_myproject/trunk
```

▶ Create a project on Beanstalk.

Visit Beanstalk, and choose Pricing & Signup and then Free Account. After signing up for an account, you should create a new Subversion repository. Use the default settings, which on Beanstalk will automatically create trunk, tags, and branches directories for you.

The trunk for your new project will be available at http://user.svn.beanstalkapp.com/myproject/trunk/.

Related Tasks

• Task 5, *Creating an Empty Project*, on page 14

37 | Migrating a CVS Repository

If you are using CVS for version control and want to upgrade to Subversion, you can do so quite easily. Subversion is designed to be a drop-in replacement for CVS; it will run on the same hardware and has a user interface similar to CVS. Subversion includes a tool called cvs2svn that allows you to convert an existing CVS repository to a Subversion repository. The tool preserves all your files, tags, branches, and history, making the upgrade pretty seamless.

Converting from a CVS repository works best on a real Unix system, so we've only included instructions for Ubuntu Linux. If you're in a real pinch, you can also try the conversion using Cygwin[15] on Windows, but we really don't recommend it. Borrow an account on a Unix box if you have to; it'll make the conversion much smoother.

The first and most important step is to make a copy of your CVS repository. Absolutely *do not* run the conversion against the primary copy of your CVS repository. cvs2svn should (in theory) only be reading files from CVS, not writing them, but you can never be too careful with your data. We'll say it again: run cvs2svn on a *copy* of your CVS repository, not the actual repository.

Converting from CVS will preserve all your history, branches, and tags. If you don't need all of that, you can run a faster conversion by specifying the --trunk-only option. Once complete, you will have a Subversion dump file containing all your CVS history. Dump files are Subversion's way of backing up a repository; you need to load the dump file into an empty Subversion repository in order to see the converted files.

The --encoding option specifies different ISO file encodings to use when trying to convert from the CVS files. The two most common are UTF8 and Latin-1. If these don't work for you, find the correct one from the full Python encodings list.[16]

---

15. http://www.cygwin.com/
16. http://docs.python.org/library/codecs.html#standard-encodings

► Install cvs2svn.

```
prompt> sudo apt-get update
prompt> sudo apt-get install cvs2svn
```

► Create a copy of your CVS repository.

```
prompt> mkdir /tmp/cvs-convert
prompt> cp -r /home/cvs/some-project /tmp/cvs-convert
```

► Convert your CVS repository to a Subversion dump file.

```
prompt> cd /tmp/cvs-convert
cvs-convert> cvs2svn --dumpfile=some-project.dump
             --encoding=UTF8 --encoding=latin1 some-project/
```

► Use the dump file to create a new repository.

```
prompt> cd /home/svn
svn> sudo mkdir some-project
svn> sudo svnadmin create some-project/
svn> sudo svnadmin load some-project/     \
             < /tmp/cvs-convert/some-project.dump
```

Related Tasks

- Task 5, *Creating an Empty Project*, on page 14

38 Backing Up and Restoring

The development team is relying on their Subversion repository to be a safe place to store all their hard work. Anyone who's worked as a systems administrator will know that disks can go bad at any time and that servers can get hacked, dropped, magnetized, and even accidentally reinstalled at any time. It's very important to have backups and to test those backups regularly.

The simplest way to create a backup is to use svnadmin dump to create a *dump file*. The dump file will contain the complete history of everything that happened to your repository—every file added, every file deleted, and every file changed. Subversion can replay this history to re-create the repository if anything bad happens to the original. Once you have created a dump file, you should store it on a different server.

Since Subversion 1.2, most repositories are simple collections of files on disk rather than something complicated like a database. In theory, if your server already has a full disk backup solution configured, your Subversion repository is also backed up. However, if someone checks in a change while the backup is running, you could end up with an inconsistent backup. To avoid this, create a dump file. Even if a check-in occurs while the dump is running, you'll end up with a consistent backup.

For large repositories, a full dump file could be quite large. You might prefer to do an incremental dump every evening and a complete dump at the weekend. The --incremental and -r REV arguments tell svnadmin to do an incremental dump starting at a particular revision. With a little bit of Unix scripting, you can create a backup regimen for your repository that does daily incremental backups and weekly complete backups. Task 39, *Performing Full Weekly Backups*, on page 118 and Task 40, *Performing Incremental Daily Backups*, on page 120 show how to accomplish this.

In addition to backing up your repository, it's a good idea to make sure it's not become corrupted over time. The svnadmin verify command will scan a repository and check whether everything is OK. This takes quite a while to run for larger repositories and will slow down the server, so you should run a verify only during off-peak hours.

► Create a Subversion dump file for your repository.

```
prompt> svnadmin dump /home/svn/mbench > mbench.dump
```

► Load the dump file to restore to a new repository.

```
prompt> svnadmin load /home/svn/mbench2 < mbench.dump
```

► Verify the integrity of a repository.

```
prompt> svnadmin verify /home/svn/mbench
```

Related Tasks

- Task 34, *Creating a Repository*, on page 108
- Task 36, *Using Third-Party Subversion Hosting*, on page 112

39 Performing Full Weekly Backups

The Subversion administrative dump and load commands are an excellent base upon which to build backup scripts for your repository. Depending on how large your repository is and the frequency with which you want to run backups, you might not always want to wait for a full backup to complete. This script and the script in the next task form a basic full and incremental backup regimen for your repository.

Most users will be comfortable running a full backup once a week and an incremental backup every day. If you are more paranoid, you could run the full backup every night and the incremental backup every hour. Some administrators even use a post-commit hook script to run an incremental backup after every check-in, but this is probably overkill most of the time.

full-backup.pl uses the svnadmin dump command to run a complete backup of the repository. The script then uses the svnlook command to determine the youngest (most recent) revision in the repository. This revision number is saved into a last-backed-up file, which the incremental backup script uses. Knowing what we have already backed up in the full backup allows the incremental backup to run much faster.

The backup script also compresses the backup using gzip. Once the backup is finished, remember to copy the backup files to a secure location such as a network drive or tape drive. Simply having some compressed dump files on the same disk as your Subversion repository isn't providing much safety!

▶ Create a full backup script for your repository.

`full-backup.pl`

```perl
#!/usr/bin/env perl
#
# Perform a full backup of a Subversion repository.

$svn_repos = "/home/svn/repos";
$backups_dir = "/home/svn/backups";

$backup_file = "full-backup." . `date +%Y%m%d%H%M%S`;
$youngest = `svnlook youngest $svn_repos`;
chomp $youngest;

print "Backing up to revision $youngest\n";
$svnadmin_cmd = "svnadmin dump --revision 0:$youngest " .
                "$svn_repos > $backups_dir/$backup_file";
`$svnadmin_cmd`;

print "Compressing dump file...\n";
print `gzip -9 $backups_dir/$backup_file`;

open(LOG, ">$backups_dir/last_backed_up");
print LOG $youngest;
close LOG;
```

▶ Run the script to perform a full backup.

```
prompt> full-backup.pl
Backing up to revision 17
* Dumped revision 0.
* Dumped revision 1.
* Dumped revision 2.
     :      :      :
* Dumped revision 17.
Compressing dump file...
```

Related Tasks

- Task 38, *Backing Up and Restoring*, on page 116
- Task 40, *Performing Incremental Daily Backups*, on the next page
- Task 42, *Using Repository Hooks*, on page 124

40 Performing Incremental Daily Backups

Building on the full backup script in the previous task, daily-backup.pl performs an incremental backup. You should run this incremental backup script at least daily, but you might run it more often if you're extra paranoid.

The script loads the last_backed_up file created by the full backup, checks to see whether there are any new revisions in the repository, and backs up just those new revisions. If there have been no check-ins since the last full backup, the script exits early and doesn't create an incremental backup. The script saves the last-backed-up revision back into last_backed_up so that future incremental backups work correctly too.

Running the script produces output such as the following:

```
prompt> daily-backup.pl
Backing up revisions 18 to 18...
* Dumped revision 18.
Compressing dump file...
```

Once your backup regimen has been running for a while, you'll have weekly full backups alongside daily incremental backups. Your /home/svn/backups directory might look like this:

```
prompt> ls -t /home/svn/backups
incremental-backup.20100517010008.gz
full-backup.20100516010011.gz
incremental-backup.20100515010002.gz
incremental-backup.20100514010004.gz
incremental-backup.20100513010011.gz
incremental-backup.20100512010008.gz
incremental-backup.20100511010003.gz
incremental-backup.20100510010011.gz
full-backup.20100509010014.gz
```

If disaster strikes and you need to restore from a backup, first use svnadmin load to load the most recent *full* backup into a new repository. Then load each subsequent *incremental* backup into the same repository. In the example shown earlier, you should load the full backup from May 16 and then load the incremental backup from May 17. All of the other backup files have been superceded by the most recent full backup and subsequent incremental backups.

► Create an incremental backup script for your repository.

daily-backup.pl

```perl
#!/usr/bin/env perl
#
# Perform an incremental backup of a Subversion repository.

$svn_repos = "/home/svn/repos";
$backups_dir = "/home/svn/backups";
$backup_file = "incremental-backup." . `date +%Y%m%d%H%M%S`;

open(IN, "$backups_dir/last_backed_up");
$previous_youngest = <IN>;
chomp $previous_youngest;
close IN;
$youngest = `svnlook youngest $svn_repos`;
chomp $youngest;

if($youngest eq $previous_youngest) {
  print "No new revisions to back up.\n";
  exit 0;
}

# We need to backup from the last backed up revision·
# to the latest (youngest) revision in the repository
$first_rev = $previous_youngest + 1;
$last_rev = $youngest;

print "Backing up revisions $first_rev to $last_rev...\n";
$svnadmin_cmd = "svnadmin dump --incremental " .
                "--revision $first_rev:$last_rev " .
                "$svn_repos > $backups_dir/$backup file";
`$svnadmin_cmd`;

print "Compressing dump file...\n";
print `gzip -9 $backups_dir/$backup_file`;

open(LOG, ">$backups_dir/last_backed_up");
print LOG $last_rev;
close LOG;
```

Related Tasks

- Task 38, *Backing Up and Restoring*, on page 116
- Task 39, *Performing Full Weekly Backups*, on page 118

41 Securing a Repository

Most organizations should use a single Subversion repository for all their projects. You should consider using multiple repositories only if you have run into a roadblock using a single repository, such as needing to support hundreds of users and not having enough room on a single server. Given that a typical Subversion repository supports multiple projects, you'll often want to limit access to each project to certain groups of users. If you're hosting your Subversion repository using Apache or svnserve, Subversion's path-based security can solve the problem.

Path-based security is enabled in Apache by including the AuthzSVNAccessFile directive for your repository. If you're using svnserve, you need to edit svnserve.conf and set the authz-db configuration property. Either way, the configuration file for path-based security has the same format.

The [groups] section allows you to define groups of users. In our example, we have defined administrators, developers, and a web development team.

Each of the subsequent configuration sections defines a path within the repository and the security we want to apply to that path. Users are specified by name or group. You can refer to all authenticated users with the special token $authenticated and to all anonymous users with $anonymous. Security for each user or group can be r for read-only access, rw for read-write access, or blank for no access.

In our example, we have security definitions for three paths in the repository. The root of the repository is writable by the administrators so they can create new projects, readable by all others users, and not accessible for anonymous users. The /mbench project directory is read-write for administrators and developers and read-only for everyone else. The /website_project directory is read-write for the web development team and not accessible for everyone else. Presumably the new corporate website is super-secret and needs to be kept locked down!

Once you have configured path-based security, you need to restart Apache for the new settings to take effect. Once Apache has restarted, you can edit dav_svn.authz to make security changes, and Subversion will notice modifications to the file and reconfigure security on the fly.

► Enable Apache's path-based security module.

Edit /etc/apache2/mods-enabled/dav_svn.conf, and ensure that for your repository the following Apache directive is uncommented:

```
AuthzSVNAccessFile /etc/apache2/dav_svn.authz
```

► Configure path-based security for your repository.

Create /etc/apache2/dav_svn.authz, and edit it to reflect the security configuration for your repository and users:

```
[groups]
admins = mike, ian
developers = mike, ian, ben
web_team = ben, natalie

[/]
admins = rw
* = r

[/mbench]
admins = rw
developers = rw
* = r

[/website_project]
web_team = rw
* =
```

► Restart Apache to enable the new configuration.

```
prompt> sudo /etc/init.d/apache2 restart
```

Related Tasks

- Task 33, *Installing Subversion Server*, on page 106
- Task 34, *Creating a Repository*, on page 108
- Task 5, *Creating an Empty Project*, on page 14

42 Using Repository Hooks

Subversion exposes a number of integration points into its transaction life cycle. These integration points are called *hooks*, and they correspond to events in the repository such as committing a change, locking and unlocking files, and altering revision properties. When Subversion gets to each point in its transaction life cycle, it will check for and execute the appropriate hook script.

Hook scripts have access to the in-flight transaction as it is being processed and are passed different command-line arguments depending on which hook script is executing. For example, the pre-commit hook is told the repository path and the transaction ID for the currently executing commit. If a hook script returns a nonzero exit code, Subversion will abort the transaction and return the script's standard error output as a message to the user.

Your repository's hooks directory contains example scripts for each hook, with a .tmpl extension. To use one of the example scripts, rename it, and drop the .tmpl extension. Windows hook scripts should have a .bat or .exe extension. The example hook scripts are an excellent resource for learning what each script should do—they are well commented and explain a lot about what's going on when the script is executed.

The following hook scripts are used most often:

pre-commit Executed before a change is committed to the repository. Often used to check log messages, to format files, and to perform custom security or policy checking.

pre-lock Executed before a lock is granted. Usually used to enforce rules around which users are allowed to lock files.

pre-unlock Executed before an unlock operation completes. Usually used to enforce rules around which users are allowed to steal locks.

post-commit Executed once the commit has completed. Often used to inform users about a completed commit, for example by sending an email to the team.

Although hook scripts have access to the transaction, they absolutely *must not* alter the content of the transaction. Some teams want to ensure all their source code is formatted to a particular standard and try to use a hook script to do the formatting. The problem with this approach is that the server has no way to inform the client that their files were modified during the commit, leading to out-of-sync working copies. The best choice in this case is to use a pre-commit hook to reject code that violates your standard, forcing a developer to reformat before they commit.

► Use a pre-commit hook to validate log messages.

Inside your repository hooks directory, create a file pre-commit with the following content:

```perl
#!/usr/bin/perl

$repos=$ARGV[0];
$txn=$ARGV[1];

$svnlook = "/usr/bin/svnlook";
$wc = "/usr/bin/wc";

$log_words = `$svnlook log -t "$txn" "$repos" | $wc -w`;
if($log_words < 1) {
  print STDERR "You must enter a log message.\n";
  exit 1;
}
exit 0;
```

Make sure the script is executable.

```
hooks> chmod +x pre-commit
```

► Use a pre-commit hook to ensure tags are read-only.

Create a pre-commit script with the following content:

```perl
#!/usr/bin/perl

$repos=$ARGV[0];
$txn=$ARGV[1];

$svnlook = "/usr/bin/svnlook";

@log_lines = `$svnlook changed -t "$txn" "$repos"`;
foreach $line (@log_lines) {
  if($line =~ /^U.*\/tags\//) {
    print STDERR "You cannot modify a tagged file.\n";
    exit 1;
  }
}
```

```
hooks> chmod +x pre-commit
```

Related Tasks

- Task 34, *Creating a Repository*, on page 108
- Task 41, *Securing a Repository*, on page 122

Part VIII

Advanced Topics

Subversion includes some advanced features that you might not need every day. Questions do often come up about these subjects, so we wanted to include extra information for advanced users.

Covered in this part:

- Subversion uses *properties* to control some of its features. One example is ignoring files using the svn:ignore property on a directory. So far we've glossed over what properties really are; Task 43, *Working with Properties*, on the following page explains the topic in full.

- Subversion's directory-based structure is flexible and free-form, with only community conventions to tell you how to structure projects inside your repository. Handling multiple projects is a common area of concern. Task 45, *Organizing Multiple Projects*, on page 134 covers a proven strategy for storing many projects in a single repository.

- Some users may want to store third-party source code inside a Subversion repository for safety in case a vendor disappears or to provide some control over the kind of third-party code that is used within their organization. If you want to properly track third-party code within your repository, you'll need to learn a few tricks, covered in this part of the book.

- Some users dealing with large files or repositories might need to work directly with the repository, bypassing a working copy. We discuss why you might want to do this, and how you should do it, in Task 47, *Working Directly with the Repository*, on page 138.

- If you have changes that you want to move around without checking in, for example via email, Task 48, *Using Patch Files*, on page 140 describes how you can do this.

43 | Working with Properties

Subversion tracks changes for directories and file contents, but it also tracks changes for *properties* attached to files and directories. Properties each have a name and text or binary content. Subversion tracks properties just like file content, so you must commit changes to properties, you can revert changes you no longer want, and it's possible for properties to be in conflict.

Subversion reserves properties whose names begin with svn: for special Subversion features. Ignoring files, enabling file locking, and setting up Subversion externals all use properties to tell Subversion how to behave. Properties can also be used by a development team if there are pieces of information that should be attached to a file but aren't part of the file's content.

The example on the facing page shows how to use a custom reviewed-by property to mark Java source code as being reviewed by another developer. When the code review is complete, we set the property to indicate who did the review. Other users can retrieve the property and see who, if anyone, reviewed the file. Of course, this isn't a very good system for doing code reviews—as soon as someone changes the file content, the review no longer applies to the new version of the file—but you can see how a team might build elements of their process around Subversion properties.

The Subversion command-line client includes a number of commands for manipulating properties. In addition to propset, propget, and propdel, proplist will list all properties on a file or directory, and propedit will fire up an editor to make changes to a property.

Tortoise provides a sophisticated graphical interface for manipulating properties. It even allows the import and export of property values so you can set a property to be binary content, such as an image. Cornerstone restricts property editing so you can only manipulate Subversion-specific properties such as svn:needs-lock.

Once you have finished altering properties, you need to commit your changes to the repository, just like file content changes. If you change your mind, you can revert a file to undo property changes. Bear in mind that reverting a file will also undo any changes to the file's contents.

► Set a text property on a file.

```
mbench> svn propset reviewed-by "mike mason: code is good"  \
                      src/mbench.java
property 'reviewed-by' set on 'src/mbench.java'
mbench> svn commit -m "Add code review comment"
```

► Retrieve a text property on a file.

```
mbench> svn propget reviewed-by src/mbench.java
mike mason - code looks good
```

► Remove a property from a file.

```
mbench> svn propdel reviewed-by src/mbench.java
property 'reviewed-by' deleted from 'src/mbench.java'.
```

► Edit a text property on a file.

```
mbench> svn propedit reviewed-by src/mbench.java
```

► Alter properties using Tortoise.

Right-click a file or directory, and choose TortoiseSVN > Properties. Use the
New..., Edit..., and Remove buttons to alter properties. Commit your changes
once you are happy with the new properties.

► Alter properties using Cornerstone.

Use the working copy browser to find the file or directory for which you
want to change properties. Ensure the Inspector panel is active, and then
click the Properties button in the Inspector panel. Alter properties, and then
commit your changes to the repository.

Related Tasks

- Task 16, *Ignoring Files*, on page 42
- Task 29, *Enabling File Locking*, on page 92
- Task 44, *Using Externals*, on the following page

44 Using Externals

Within an organization, it's quite likely that development teams will want to share assets between projects. It might be a goal for projects to use a common set of third-party components or for certain projects to share parts of their source code for other projects to use. Subversion's *externals* provide an easy way to include portions of a repository within a project.

Externals are controlled through the svn:externals property, which can be set on any directory within a repository. When a Subversion client sees the external, it attempts to contact the specified Subversion repository and check out a portion of that repository into the working copy. An external can refer to a directory or a single file that you want to include in your working copy. Once you have set svn:externals on a directory, doing an update causes the Subversion client to pull in the extra directories or files.

svn:externals is a multiline property with each line specifying a source URL for the external and a target directory in the working copy. Source URLs can be absolute or relative; you should always use a relative URL if you are referring to the current repository.

Relative URLs always refer to the repository in which the external is defined, and they're especially useful when a repository has multiple access methods or names. For example, on my machine, I might refer to http://svn.mycompany.com/mbench, and you might refer to https://svn/mbench. Both these URLs point to the same repository—which one is right to use in an external? Subversion solves this problem by providing the following relative URL definitions:

../   Relative to the directory on which svn:externals is set

^/   Relative to the root of the repository in which svn:externals is set

//   Relative to the scheme of the URL of the directory on which svn:externals is set

/   Relative to the root URL of the server on which svn:externals is set

In our example, we use ^/libraries to mean the libraries directory in the root of the current repository. Clients using different access schemes such as svn, http, and https will all translate the external correctly.

Once you have made a change to svn:externals, as with any other property change, you must commit to the repository before anyone else will see the new externals.

▶ Add libraries to your project using externals.

Use svn propedit or the Tortoise or Cornerstone GUI to edit the svn:externals property on the base directory of your project.

```
^/libraries/MongoDB/1.4 libraries/mongo
```

Run an update to ensure the new external works as you expect, and then commit your changes to the repository.

```
mongo> svn update
Fetching external item into 'libraries/mongo'
A    libraries/mongo/mongo.jar
Updated external to revision 25.

Updated to revision 25.
mongo> svn commit -m "Pulled in Mongo 1.4 library"
```

▶ Add third-party code to your project using externals.

Use svn propedit or the Tortoise or Cornerstone GUI to edit the svn:externals property on the base directory of your project.

```
http://svn.apache.org/repos/asf/subversion/trunk/notes/
   dependencies/subversion
```

Run an update to ensure the new external works as you expect, and then commit your changes to the repository.

```
mongo> svn update
Fetching external item into 'dependencies/subversion'
A    dependencies/subversion/repos_upgrade_HOWTO
A    dependencies/subversion/sasl.txt
A    dependencies/subversion/svnsync.txt
     :    :    :
A    dependencies/subversion/wc-ng/transitions
A    dependencies/subversion/asp-dot-net-hack.txt
Updated external to revision 947760.

Updated to revision 25.
mongo> svn commit -m "Added Subversion notes as dependencies"
```

Related Tasks

- Task 43, *Working with Properties*, on page 130
- Task 45, *Organizing Multiple Projects*, on the following page

45 Organizing Multiple Projects

One of the most common questions asked by teams new to Subversion is, "How can we host multiple projects within a repository?" Subversion uses directories to organize projects, and directories are also used to store tags and branches, so there are many different project structures that can work.

The simplest organization strategy is to have a root-level directory for each project. Within each project directory, you should create the usual trunk, tags, and branches subdirectories. Each project is then free to evolve independently, branching and creating release tags as they see fit. If you want to share artifacts between projects, you can use Subversion externals to include directories from one project inside another project. You might do this if one of the projects is a utility designed to be shared across projects.

More complex organization schemes are possible. One common question is around dependent projects that need to have a similar life cycle, for example components of a services ecosystem. These components are interdependent, so you might put them all inside a single trunk directory and then branch and tag them as a unit. This approach can work but is usually a mistake—as soon as one of the components wants to evolve at a different rate than the others, the model is broken.

If you are using externals to share code or libraries between projects, you need to take extra care when dealing with release branches. On a release branch, we want to be able to re-create the exact state of the code and any dependencies, but an external that references the *trunk* of another project can change over time. On a release branch, always update your externals so that they point to a tagged release from another project, or use *pegged revisions*[17] for all your externals.

When deciding on how to structure your Subversion repository, make sure to think about the kinds of projects you want to store, whether those projects have interdependencies, and how the projects evolve over time. Try a few thought experiments to see how branching, releasing, and bug fixing would work with your structure. Finally, make sure both developers and Subversion administrators understand your organization strategy.

---

17. http://svnbook.red-bean.com/en/1.5/svn.advanced.externals.html

▶ Create repository directories for your projects.

In the root of your repository, create a base directory for each project. Inside each project directory, create trunk, tags, and branches subdirectories.

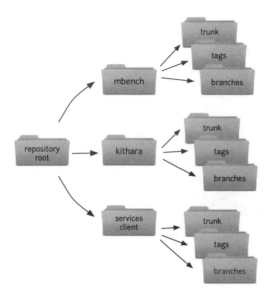

▶ Use externals to share code or other artifacts between projects.

If one of your projects is creating a shared library for use by other projects, use svn:externals to include part of a project inside another project.

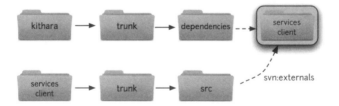

Related Tasks

- Task 5, *Creating an Empty Project*, on page 14
- Task 44, *Using Externals*, on page 132

46 | Storing Third-Party Code

Most third-party libraries are distributed in binary format, usually as a .dll or .jar file that you can link directly into your project. Some vendors provide source code in addition to binaries, and it can be useful to track that source code yourself. If the vendor ever goes away, you'll still have all the source code and will be able to make changes and bug fixes to the library.

You should store all your vendor source code in one place in your repository. In the instructions on the facing page, we put all vendor code in named directories beneath /vendorsrc. Start by unzipping the source code (sometimes called a *code drop*) to a temporary directory. Next, import the code drop into a current directory inside the repository. We'll use the current directory for future code drops. Finally, create a tag for the release. When other projects want to use the third-party source code, they should always use a tagged version, never current.

When a new version of the library becomes available, we need to update our current version to match the new code drop. We're trying to mimic inside Subversion what would have happened during the vendor's development of a new release. The vendor has probably added files, removed files, and updated file content. To mimic this, we might check out a working copy of current and then unzip the new code drop over the top. This would give us a working copy with all the updated files, but it wouldn't help us with files that the vendor added or removed in the new code drop. Manually figuring out how to sync a working copy of current with a new code drop is a lot of work.

Fortunately, there's a Python tool that does all the heavy lifting for us. svn-load is available online[18] and requires the Python Subversion bindings. If you're using Ubuntu, run apt-get install svn-load to install svn-load and its dependencies.

Unzip the new code drop in a temporary directory. Run svn-load, telling it the new tag version you'd like to apply, the URL for the current directory, and the location of the new code drop on your local machine. svn-load will automatically figure out which files have been added, removed, or changed by the vendor. svn-load will update the current directory in the repository and tag it with the new version number. Teams can then update their projects and use the new release.

---

18. http://free.linux.hp.com/~dannf/svn-load/

▶ Import third-party source code.

Extract the third-party source code to a temporary directory. Here we use /temp/NUnit-2.5.0.

```
temp> svn import -m "Import NUnit 2.5.0"  NUnit-2.5.0 \
      http://svn.mycompany.com/vendorsrc/nunit/current
Adding          NUnit-2.5.0/NUnitTests.config
Adding          NUnit-2.5.0/NUnitFitTests.html
   :     :     :
Adding          NUnit-2.5.0/install/NUnit.wxs
Adding          NUnit-2.5.0/license.rtf
```

▶ Create a tagged version of the third-party code.

```
temp> svn copy -m "Tag 2.5.0 vendor drop" \
      http://svn.mycompany.com/vendorsrc/nunit/current  \
      http://svn.mycompany.com/vendorsrc/nunit/2.5.0
Committed revision 29.
```

▶ Update to a new third-party release.

Extract the new code drop to a temporary directory. Here we use /temp/NUnit-2.5.5.

```
temp> svn-load -t 2.5.5 http://svn.mycompany.com/vendorsrc/nunit  \
                        current NUnit-2.5.5
      Deleted                               Added
  0 doc/img/assemblyReloadOptions.JPG___   doc/assemblyIsolation.html
  1 doc/img/testResultOptions.JPG_____  doc/runningTests.html
  2 doc/img/textOutputOptions.jpg_____  doc/runtimeSelection.html
   :       :      :
Enter two indexes for each column to rename,
(R)elist, or (F)inish: F
```

Related Tasks

- Task 6, *Creating a Project from an Existing Source Tree*, on page 16
- Task 28, *Tagging a Release*, on page 84

47 Working Directly with the Repository

Most of the time you should make changes to a Subversion working copy and then commit those changes to the repository. This gives you a chance to think about the changes, revert unwanted or erroneous modifications, and even run a build to make sure everything works before you commit. There are times, though, when you might want to work directly with the repository. For some Subversion commands, you can use a repository URL instead of referring to working copy files.

You can copy, move, rename, and delete items directly in the repository. You might want to do this if the files are large and would take a long time to manipulate in a working copy. You might also want to do this if you recently imported a large number of files and need to rearrange them. If developers are working on files when they are moved, Subversion will report a tree conflict when they attempt to commit their changes. If a user has a file locked, it cannot be moved, renamed, or deleted within the repository until the lock is released.

Subversion stores history forever. In our example, we're deleting a password file that someone has accidentally added to the repository. Deleting a file only removes it from Subversion's "current" view of what's in the repository. If someone knows that the password file is there, they can go back in time using Subversion's history features and retrieve the file. If you do accidentally commit confidential information to a Subversion repository, you will have to do a lot of work to really remove the data by dumping the repository and then reloading it using svndumpfilter to filter out the confidential file.[19] The dump/load process can be quite time-consuming and will involve downtime on the repository. Be careful what you commit!

---

19. http://svnbook.red-bean.com/en/1.5/svn.reposadmin.html has more information about the svndumpfilter command.

► Copy an item directly on the repository.

```
mbench> svn cp http://svn.mycompany.com/mbench/trunk/lib/mongo-1.4.jar \
               http://svn.mycompany.com/libraries/mongo \
               -m "Copy Mongo jar to shared libraries directory"
```

► Rename an item directly on the repository.

```
mbench> svn mv http://svn.mycompany.com/mbench/trunk/docs \
               http://svn.mycompany.com/mbench/trunk/documentation \
               -m "Renaming to make us look more professional"
```

► Delete an item from the repository.

```
mbench> svn rm http://svn.mycompany.com/mbench/trunk/config/passwd \
               -m "Removing accidentally added password file"
```

► Rename a repository item using Tortoise.

Right-click in your project working copy, and choose TortoiseSVN >
Repo-browser. Navigate to the item you want to rename, right-click it, and
choose Rename. Type a new name for the item, and press Enter.

Enter a log message explaining the reason for the change, and then click OK
to complete the change.

► Rename a repository item using Cornerstone.

Select your repository from the repository source list. Using the repository
browser, navigate to the item you want to rename. Select the item, pause for
a second, and then click the item name again to make it editable. Type a new
name for the item, and press Enter.

Enter a log message explaining the reason for the change, and then click
Continue to complete the change.

Related Tasks

- Task 13, *Removing Files and Directories*, on page 36
- Task 14, *Moving and Renaming Files and Directories*, on page 38

48 Using Patch Files

Occasionally you might want to save a copy of your working copy changes without committing them to the repository. You might decide your changes aren't yet ready for prime time and that you want to keep them for later (although in this case, creating a feature branch and checking in to the branch is safer). Alternatively, you might be working on an open source project on the Internet and not have commit access to the repository. Instead of committing your changes directly, you need to send them to someone else on the project who has commit access.

Patch files are the Unix world's solution to this problem. A patch file is a description of changes you have made to some files. You can send the patch file to someone else who has the original files, and they can *apply* the patch to get your changes. Patch files include a special syntax that often allows them to work even if the person you're sending the patch to doesn't have exactly the same revision of the files as were used to create the patch.

Subversion's diff command shows working copy modifications in "unified diff" format so you can create a patch file by saving svn diff results to a file. Tortoise and Cornerstone allow you to select a file or directory and save any modifications to a patch file.

Once you have a patch file, you can send it to someone else or keep it somewhere safe for your own use. To apply a patch file, use the Unix patch command or the Tortoise or Cornerstone "apply patch" functionality. Applying a patch takes the changes described in the patch file and attempts to perform them on another set of files. For our purposes, this should always be another Subversion working copy.

If the patch does not apply cleanly, it's usually because the new working copy where the patch is being applied has a different revision of the files than were used to create the patch. The various different patch tools handle this in different ways.

The command-line and Cornerstone clients both use the Unix patch command to apply patches. If a patch can't be applied successfully, patch saves rejected "hunks" to a copy of the file with a .rej suffix. You can look at the reject files and attempt to resolve the conflicts yourself. If Tortoise can't apply a patch cleanly, you can use the TortoiseMerge tool to resolve conflicts, as described in Task 19, *Handling Conflicts Using Tortoise*, on page 54.

▶ Create a patch file using the command-line client.

```
mbench> svn diff > mychanges.patch
```

▶ Apply a patch file using the command-line client.

```
mbench2> patch < mychanges.patch
```

▶ Create a patch file using Tortoise.

Right-click the base directory for your working copy, and choose TortoiseSVN > Create patch.... Select the files you want to include in the patch, and click OK.

Specify a file in which to save the patch, and then click Save. Tortoise will create the patch file, save it to disk, and then display it in a graphical browser.

▶ Apply a patch file using Tortoise.

Right-click the base directory for your working copy, and choose TortoiseSVN > Apply patch.... Browse to your patch file, select it, and click Open.

Tortoise will open two windows, one listing the files in the patch and the other a large TortoiseMerge window. For each file to be patched, double-click the filename to apply the changes in the merge window. If you're happy that the changes applied correctly, press Ctrl+S to save the changes.

▶ Create a patch file using Cornerstone.

Select your working copy from the working copy sources list. Click the File menu, and choose Save Differences in "mbench" as Patch.... Enter a filename, and click Save to create the patch file.

▶ Apply a patch file using Cornerstone.

Select your working copy from the working copy sources list. Click the File menu, and choose Apply Patch to "mbench2".... Browse to your patch file, and click Apply.

Related Tasks

- Task 8, *Seeing What You've Changed*, on page 26
- Task 11, *Committing Changes*, on page 32

Bibliography

[Mas06]   Mike Mason. *Pragmatic Version Control Using Subversion.*
           The Pragmatic Programmers, LLC, Raleigh, NC, and Dallas,
           TX, second edition, 2006.

[Swi08]   Travis Swicegood. *Pragmatic Version Control using Git.* The
           Pragmatic Programmers, LLC, Raleigh, NC, and Dallas, TX,
           2008.

Index

The Pragmatic Bookshelf

Available in paperback and DRM-free eBooks, our titles are here to help you stay on top of your game. The following are in print as of October 2010; be sure to check our website at pragprog.com for newer titles.

Title	Year	ISBN	Pages
Advanced Rails Recipes: 84 New Ways to Build Stunning Rails Apps	2008	9780978739225	464
Agile Coaching	2009	9781934356432	248
Agile Retrospectives: Making Good Teams Great	2006	9780977616640	200
Agile Web Development with Rails	2009	9781934356166	792
Beginning Mac Programming: Develop with Objective-C and Cocoa	2010	9781934356517	300
Behind Closed Doors: Secrets of Great Management	2005	9780976694021	192
Best of Ruby Quiz	2006	9780976694076	304
Cocoa Programming: A Quick-Start Guide for Developers	2010	9781934356302	450
Core Animation for Mac OS X and the iPhone: Creating Compelling Dynamic User Interfaces	2008	9781934356104	200
Core Data: Apple's API for Persisting Data on Mac OS X	2009	9781934356326	256
Data Crunching: Solve Everyday Problems using Java, Python, and More	2005	9780974514079	208
Debug It! Find, Repair, and Prevent Bugs in Your Code	2009	9781934356289	232
Deploying Rails Applications: A Step-by-Step Guide	2008	9780978739201	280
Design Accessible Web Sites: 36 Keys to Creating Content for All Audiences and Platforms	2007	9781934356029	336
Desktop GIS: Mapping the Planet with Open Source Tools	2008	9781934356067	368
Domain-Driven Design Using Naked Objects	2009	9781934356449	375
Enterprise Integration with Ruby	2006	9780976694069	360
Enterprise Recipes with Ruby and Rails	2008	9781934356234	416
Everyday Scripting with Ruby: for Teams, Testers, and You	2007	9780977616619	320
ExpressionEngine 2: A Quick-Start Guide	2010	9781934356524	250
From Java To Ruby: Things Every Manager Should Know	2006	9780976694090	160
FXRuby: Create Lean and Mean GUIs with Ruby	2008	9781934356074	240
GIS for Web Developers: Adding Where to Your Web Applications	2007	9780974514093	275
Google Maps API: Adding Where to Your Applications	2006	PDF-Only	83
Grails: A Quick-Start Guide	2009	9781934356463	200
Groovy Recipes: Greasing the Wheels of Java	2008	9780978739294	264
Hello, Android: Introducing Google's Mobile Development Platform	2010	9781934356562	320

Continued on next page

Title	Year	ISBN	Pages
Interface Oriented Design	2006	9780976694052	240
iPad Programming: A Quick-Start Guide for iPhone Developers	2010	9781934356579	248
iPhone SDK Development	2009	9781934356258	576
Land the Tech Job You Love	2009	9781934356265	280
Language Implementation Patterns: Create Your Own Domain-Specific and General Programming Languages	2009	9781934356456	350
Learn to Program	2009	9781934356364	240
Manage It! Your Guide to Modern Pragmatic Project Management	2007	9780978739249	360
Manage Your Project Portfolio: Increase Your Capacity and Finish More Projects	2009	9781934356296	200
Mastering Dojo: JavaScript and Ajax Tools for Great Web Experiences	2008	9781934356111	568
Metaprogramming Ruby: Program Like the Ruby Pros	2010	9781934356470	240
Modular Java: Creating Flexible Applications with OSGi and Spring	2009	9781934356401	260
No Fluff Just Stuff 2006 Anthology	2006	9780977616664	240
No Fluff Just Stuff 2007 Anthology	2007	9780978739287	320
Pomodoro Technique Illustrated: The Easy Way to Do More in Less Time	2009	9781934356500	144
Practical Programming: An Introduction to Computer Science Using Python	2009	9781934356272	350
Practices of an Agile Developer	2006	9780974514086	208
Pragmatic Guide to Git	2010	9781934356722	168
Pragmatic Project Automation: How to Build, Deploy, and Monitor Java Applications	2004	9780974514031	176
Pragmatic Thinking and Learning: Refactor Your Wetware	2008	9781934356050	288
Pragmatic Unit Testing in C# with NUnit	2007	9780977616671	176
Pragmatic Unit Testing in Java with JUnit	2003	9780974514017	160
Pragmatic Version Control using CVS	2003	9780974514000	176
Pragmatic Version Control Using Git	2008	9781934356159	200
Pragmatic Version Control using Subversion	2006	9780977616657	248
Programming Clojure	2009	9781934356333	304
Programming Cocoa with Ruby: Create Compelling Mac Apps Using RubyCocoa	2009	9781934356197	300
Programming Erlang: Software for a Concurrent World	2007	9781934356005	536
Programming Groovy: Dynamic Productivity for the Java Developer	2008	9781934356098	320
Programming Ruby: The Pragmatic Programmers' Guide	2004	9780974514055	864
Programming Ruby 1.9: The Pragmatic Programmers' Guide	2009	9781934356081	960

Continued on next page

Title	Year	ISBN	Pages
Programming Scala: Tackle Multi-Core Complexity on the Java Virtual Machine	2009	9781934356319	250
Prototype and script.aculo.us: You Never Knew JavaScript Could Do This!	2007	9781934356012	448
Rails for .NET Developers	2008	9781934356203	300
Rails for Java Developers	2007	9780977616695	336
Rails for PHP Developers	2008	9781934356043	432
Rails Recipes	2006	9780977616602	350
Rapid GUI Development with QtRuby	2005	PDF-Only	83
Release It! Design and Deploy Production-Ready Software	2007	9780978739218	368
Scripted GUI Testing with Ruby	2008	9781934356180	192
Seven Languages in Seven Weeks: A Pragmatic Guide to Learning Programming Languages	2010	9781934356593	300
Ship It! A Practical Guide to Successful Software Projects	2005	9780974514048	224
SQL Antipatterns: Avoiding the Pitfalls of Database Programming	2010	9781934356555	352
Stripes ...and Java Web Development Is Fun Again	2008	9781934356210	375
Test-Drive ASP.NET MVC	2010	9781934356531	296
TextMate: Power Editing for the Mac	2007	9780978739232	208
The Agile Samurai: How Agile Masters Deliver Great Software	2010	9781934356586	280
The Definitive ANTLR Reference: Building Domain-Specific Languages	2007	9780978739256	384
The Passionate Programmer: Creating a Remarkable Career in Software Development	2009	9781934356340	200
ThoughtWorks Anthology	2008	9781934356142	240
Ubuntu Kung Fu: Tips, Tricks, Hints, and Hacks	2008	9781934356227	400
Web Design for Developers: A Programmer's Guide to Design Tools and Techniques	2009	9781934356135	300

The Pragmatic Bookshelf

The Pragmatic Bookshelf features books written by developers for developers. The titles continue the well-known Pragmatic Programmer style and continue to garner awards and rave reviews. As development gets more and more difficult, the Pragmatic Programmers will be there with more titles and products to help you stay on top of your game.

Visit Us Online

Pragmatic Guide to Subversion
http://pragprog.com/titles/pg_svn
Source code from this book, errata, and other resources. Come give us feedback, too!

Register for Updates
http://pragprog.com/updates
Be notified when updates and new books become available.

Join the Community
http://pragprog.com/community
Read our weblogs, join our online discussions, participate in our mailing list, interact with our wiki, and benefit from the experience of other Pragmatic Programmers.

New and Noteworthy
http://pragprog.com/news
Check out the latest pragmatic developments, new titles and other offerings.

Save on the eBook

Save on the eBook versions of this title. Owning the paper version of this book entitles you to purchase the electronic versions at a terrific discount.

PDFs are great for carrying around on your laptop—they are hyperlinked, have color, and are fully searchable. Most titles are also available for the iPhone and iPod touch, Amazon Kindle, and other popular e-book readers.

Buy now at pragprog.com/coupon.

Contact Us

Online Orders:	www.pragprog.com/catalog
Customer Service:	support@pragprog.com
Non-English Versions:	translations@pragprog.com
Pragmatic Teaching:	academic@pragprog.com
Author Proposals:	proposals@pragprog.com
Contact us:	1-800-699-PROG (+1 919 847 3884)